Serve Better Thy Country

- How to Write Winning Essays to Prestigious Colleges

An insider's guide to crafting exceptional essays for your University of California, Common App, and Coalition applications

With In-Depth Analysis from the Experts at

Ivy Club USA

DEDICATION

To every student preparing to embark on the distresses, disappointments, and ultimate triumphs of his or her college application adventure.

ACKNOWLEDGMENTS

We are eternally grateful to Dr. William Miller, former Stanford University Vice President and Provost, for his guidance and inspiration that laid the foundation for our work -- and, consequently, this book. From 2007 to 2010, Dr. Miller travelled with our team in the U.S. and overseas to help us instill in college-bound young people a sense of mission and responsibility for local communities and society at large. That same spirit has guided our work with middle school, high school, and college students in their pursuit of educational opportunities at every level. It is those students' successes over the past two decades that led to the writing of this book. We are thankful that Ivy Club USA is publishing this book to guide future students in their college pursuits and, more importantly, to inspire that sense of duty in these young people, especially as the COVID-19 pandemic ravages the world's state of affairs.

A very special thanks goes to Professor Kaiping Peng, PhD, Department of Psychology at the University of California, Berkeley and Founding Dean of Tsinghua University's School of Social Sciences, for his invaluable insights on positive psychology and its impact on youth mental health, as well as his support for our humanitarian projects, such as the P2P Microfinance Poverty Alleviation and the Sustainable Environmental Engineering projects in China, through which generations of Ivy Club students learned and grew over the years. So many of our students drew inspiration from these experiences in their successful college application essays. But as Professor Peng keenly observed, these mission-minded young people have also returned to many of these underdeveloped but improving areas, equipped with newfound wisdom and skills from their college education, to better serve those people in need.

We would also like to thank our editors, Dr. Trevor Chen, Dr. Gary Lemco, Dr. Angela Garbin, Sebastian Montes, and other Ivy Club USA colleagues for their critical editing and constructive suggestions throughout the writing process; and to our design team, especially

Jerry Yeh and Beatrice Cao, for their creative expertise in designing the layout and cover, as well as their patience in producing the numerous revisions of this book.

ADDITIONAL ACKNOWLEDGEMENT FROM SHIN WEI, THE FOUNDER OF IVY CLUB USA:

I want to thank my parents, Marlene and Jack, who were wise and courageous enough to set sail my solo journey to America in 1980, which led to my high school struggles in San Francisco, college triumph at the University of Pennsylvania, consulting work on Wall Street, to high-tech startup success in Silicon Valley, Ivy Club adventures both in the U.S. and overseas, and finally this book's birth. I am also deeply indebted to my wife and co-founder, Vickie Zhang, without whose never-failing encouragement this book would still be stuck in conceptual stages. Last but not least, thank you to my children, Austin and Jocelyn, who put together that first IKEA bookshelf for our students in 2004, upon which this book will become another proud addition.

CONTENTS

Introduction

The Harvard University report on the state of college admissions, published in early 2016, presented a highly critical view of the current generation's "herd mentality" and single-minded pursuit of admission to the top-tier universities. Led by Harvard and other Ivy League schools, more than 100 of the nation's leading universities are seeking to overhaul that whole admissions process by "Turning the Tide: Inspiring Concern for Others and the Common Good through College Admissions."

Ostensibly, the "best" students should gain admission into the best colleges and universities. The primary job of admission officers is to determine who qualify as the best applicants and reward them with entry into their selective schools. Distinctions such as admission to honors programs and merit-based scholarships continue this evaluative process to a further extent. However, as evidenced by admissions data and Harvard's "Turning the Tide" report, the job of deciding who deserves the "honor of admission" to top-tier colleges in the U.S. has become increasingly *holistic* and *subjective*. The rates of admission at Harvard and Stanford steadily move below the 5% mark. Top schools do not want only students with perfect grades and stellar test scores. They now seek someone else.

Thus, college essays and descriptions of a student's activities assume greater importance than ever. The goal of holistic admissions showcases the student as a *whole person*. Admissions officers want to answer the question: "Who is the student really, beyond a collection of numbers like their GPA and SAT/AP test scores?" Learning how to answer this question distinctively through *the written word* lies at the heart of this book. Adolescence presents a time when most students seek to be an accepted part of social groups; thus, this challenge of self-disclosure can be especially difficult for teenagers.

Going beyond the numbers becomes even more important in the case of Asian-American students because applying to U.S. colleges does not always present an even playing field for the "Model Minority." For starters, everyone assumes, based upon stereotypes and widely publicized statistics, that Asian-American students perform better at mathematics and the sciences than do their counterparts from other ethnic groups. But, ultimately, this prejudice becomes more of a challenge to these students, because admissions officers assume Asian Americans already possess these skills. Asian-American students, ironically, compete as adversaries against each other for spots in freshman classes bounded by quotas, caps and other limitations, based on their ethnicity.

With few exceptions, top-tier undergraduate schools rarely allow Asian Americans to comprise more than 20% of their freshman classes. Many of the nation's top schools admit significantly lower numbers, despite presumably large Asian-American applicant pools: Cornell (16%), Dartmouth (14%), Brown (12%), Boston College (10%), Tufts (10%), Georgetown (9%), Northeastern (9%), Vanderbilt (8%), Notre Dame (7%), College of William and Mary (6%), et al. Among liberal arts colleges, this "cap" seems to be even lower – around 10%: Amherst (12%), Pomona (11%), Claremont McKenna (11%), Williams (11%), Haverford (10%), Bowdoin (7%), Middlebury (6%), et al. (Source: *The Best 378 Colleges, 2014 Edition*).

Ultimately, these numbers tend to indicate that it has never been more competitive for qualified Asian-American students to attend top schools because their "slice of the admissions pie" remains relatively small. This situation suffers further exacerbation from groups admitted under special considerations, such as legacy, first-generation, lower-income students, and other institutional priorities. Typically, Asians do not fall into these special categories, further reducing the slots available. Some believe that international students may be granted greater chances of admission because such candidates assume that they will pay full or increased tuition, but this idea often proves fallacious. With the exception of less-selective public schools, international students will find themselves competing for even fewer spots against literally "the whole world"—an applicant pool that includes talents from around the globe.

Now that we have thoroughly intimidated you with statistics, it is time we return to the main theme of this book: demonstrating one's concern for others and the common good and the important role one's application essays play in such a process.

This book offers a unique resource written from real-world examples of our work with Asian and Asian-American students. From general topics such as "Narrative Writing" and "What Is And Is Not a College Essay," to more specific discussions on "When to Ignore Popular Advice," "Making the Small Meaningful," and "Making the Epic Intimate," this book presents detailed advice on how to write winning essays for top-tier colleges. Our expert counselors and editors also share their insights about a collection of successful students' application essays to some of the most selective and competitive schools, including Harvard, Princeton, Yale, Stanford, and MIT.

However, this book does not intend to replace consultation with experienced counselors and editors—there exists no substitute for expert assistance—but rather to complement these services by providing examples to set students upon the right track. More importantly, writing the successful essay merely sets the stage for personal success: Asian-American students should focus more of their efforts on passionately pursuing their interests, academic or otherwise, and paying attention to real-world problems. Demonstrating their genuine concerns for something larger than themselves, and continuing their quest for developing sustainable solutions to these problems will help shape their minds to consider the greater good. While aiming beyond college, not simply at college, these Asian-American students with big hearts will naturally become much more qualified candidates for the top-tier schools—with their winning essays, of course.

- Shin Wei, Founder, Ivy Club USA

About the Authors

Helen "The Professor"

Helen is a Phi Beta Kappa, Magna Cum Laude graduate of Harvard University, which she attended as a National Merit Scholar. Helen has worked for Ivy Club USA for fifteen years as teacher, coach, and editor, and in the process, positively impacted hundreds of students' college admissions. As one of the most famous SAT instructors at the Ivy Club, Helen has coached students to gains of 200-600 points on their test scores, with many of them scoring perfect SAT's over the last decade. Prior to teaching at the Ivy Club, Helen served as principal of the Middle School at St. Anne's, the largest division of an exclusive private school in New York City, named by the Wall Street Journal in 2004 as the Most Successful School at gaining admissions to the most prestigious colleges in the U.S. She also enjoyed a short but highly successful career in venture capital investments in Silicon Valley before returning her focus to education.

John "The Environmentalist"

John has an MA in Urban Planning and Design from the UCLA, and a BA in Sociology from Wesleyan University. Before working for Ivy Club USA, John taught English at a Spanish-English bilingual charter school in St. Paul, MN, and served as the national training director for student-run activities for the Sierra Club. Over the last five years, John has helped Ivy Club students gain admission into top-tier colleges, specializing in the Ivy Leagues and liberal arts colleges such as Williams, Amherst, Pomona, Carlton, Swarthmore, Claremont McKenna, Wesleyan, Grinnell, and others. His expertise in environmental policy and design has uniquely and significantly enhanced his students' chances of getting into some of the top-tier programs in environmental engineering, environmental science, and environmental studies.

Matthew "The Idealist"

Matthew graduated from the UC Berkeley with a BA in English Literature and an MFA degree from the University of New Mexico. He has taught college classes on the poetics of imagination, oral poetics, eco-poetics, Western film and literature, English composition, and expository writing. Since joining Ivy Club USA, Matthew has continued to teach and inspire students from middle schools and high schools to reach their dream colleges.

Michael "The Rising Star"

Michael is a full-time editor, counselor, instructor, and public speaking coach with Ivy Club USA. Before joining the Ivy Club, Michael attended UC Berkeley, where he earned a BA in Rhetoric. While at Berkeley, he competed in Collegiate Policy Debate, a research-based, team debate style that emphasizes quality evidence, creative argumentation, and effective presentation. He has gained years of coaching experience as an instructor for the Cal National Debate Institute and a coach for the Bay Area Urban Debate League. His academic background and speech coaching experience make him a highly effective editor and instructor.

Ren-Horng "The Hollywood Writer"

Ren-Horng holds a Masters of Public Administration from Ohio State University and a double-AB in Art-Semiotics and Geology-Biology from Brown University. Over the last two decades, Ren-Horng has not only traveled to remote locales around the world for poverty-focused philanthropic efforts, but also led numerous student groups to work on sustainable environmental development projects in Nepal and China. Prior to joining Ivy Club USA, Ren-Horng worked for AmeriCorp to rebuild the Gulf Coast following Hurricane Katrina, as well as the global education program Up with People to shape young people's character via meaningful community service activities. At the Ivy Club, he has helped hundreds of students gain admission to Ivy League schools,

Stanford, MIT, Caltech, Northwestern, NYU, USC, Pomona, Wellesley, UC Berkeley, UCLA, and many others. In addition to being an inspirational teacher and editor to Ivy Club students, Ren-Horng has also written scripts for award-winning Hollywood short films.

Welcome to the College Application Process

by Ren-Horng "The Hollywood Writer"

Applying to college can seem like an overwhelming process, but breaking down the components of what colleges are looking for in an applicant can make the college application process more manageable. This section identifies the parts of a student's profile that colleges look at and why it's important to write memorable, distinctive essays.

The clock is ticking

Senior year is about to begin, or maybe the fall is already in full swing. You know you're applying to college, but maybe you don't know where to start yet. Perhaps you might also be bogged down by classes, homework, standardized tests—all of which are understandable—but time stops for no one. By November (in some cases, even October!), your first college applications will be due.

Don't be caught ill-prepared! Now is the time to do exploratory research of the task that lies ahead of you. You can find applications to the colleges you want to apply to online and register for an account. After you do and log in, you will find a myriad of forms to fill out that ask questions ranging from where you were born to where your parents went to college to what classes you will be taking spring of senior year. But you're not done there! There's also an activities section to fill out and then the additional, custom-tailored-per-school short answers and essays that the colleges want you to write.

The University of California alone requires four essays. By applying to another five top colleges, you will add at least another six essays, one common one and at least one school-specific essay for each of the five schools, but realistically, some of these schools will ask two, three, or even eight questions in addition to the common essay. With ten schools, a student is looking at twenty or more essays and short answers to write. How will this all get done? Take a deep breath. Don't panic. We're here to help.

College application overview

In a college application, a college seeks to know more about you, the student applicant. The application therefore compiles basic information about you and lays it out for the colleges by categorizing you in these areas:

- GPA, course rigor of classes chosen
- SAT, SAT II, ACT scores
- Extracurricular Activities
- Personal Statement(s)

Some colleges will also ask for these in addition to the above bullet points:

- Recommendations
- Interviews

Now, looking at this list of factors that colleges look at when they make admissions decisions, you might think that this formula is reductive and doesn't allow you to present your best, full self. You are right. After all, what are GPA and standardized test scores other than numbers that are used to compare you with numbers from other people? Factor in the fact that students with good test scores and high GPAs are at every school, and that you probably have known students with great statistics who *didn't* get into their dream schools, you may start to wonder, *what is it* in an applicant that colleges look for?

They look for the things that make you a real person

Much of how you are perceived as a real person will come down to extracurriculars, personal statements, recommendations, and interviews. As far as the University of California system goes, however, recommendations and interviews are only factors in special cases. Furthermore, extracurriculars also have their own limitations, as many high schools have the same clubs and many students have the same activities. That is why your personal statements are especially important when it comes to differentiating you from your competition. If you want to make an impression on your reader, then your essay must be:

- Memorable (for the right reasons)
- Relevant/on topic
- Revealing/about you

How to use this book

This book will focus on giving you every advantage in the essay portion of your application. Tips on how your essay can have the qualities mentioned above, no matter your chosen topic, will be explored throughout this volume. Every chapter will cover a different technique and (for those of you who like to flip back and forth) will be laid out with short summaries at the beginning and end of each chapter. Every chapter is also broken down by subheadings to help you find the points most relevant to wherever you are in your writing journey.

So, future college students, have no fear, you have picked up the right book! Our seasoned team of editors will guide you through the process, and soon you'll be on your way to writing a winning essay.

But also keep in mind...

Having one or more great essays will definitely give you an advantage in the college admissions process, but it is not the only factor. Be sure to read the directions on the application not only on the application platform itself, but also on the college's website. Sometimes colleges will have extra instructions (such as providing a portfolio, scheduling an interview, and even special, *early* deadlines) for their application not expressly stated on the application itself.

Furthermore, some schools are notorious for having hidden essays that are either not labeled as writing supplements or are only unlocked once you have picked your major. Just because the application platform itself says that a college does not have a writing supplement does not mean that there isn't one!

You could write a fantastic essay, but not following the directions on the college website, having a poor recommendation, or not preparing for the school interview can sink your chances of admission. It would be terrible to miss the opportunity to gain admission to your dream college because you did not read the fine print on the college's website! Therefore, it is most important to fill out the application completely and with great care to maximize the chances of being admitted to your dream school.

Bringing it all together

When colleges consider whom to admit, they look at GPA, classes taken, standardized test scores, extracurricular activities, personal statements, and sometimes recommendations and interviews. Because so many students have high GPAs and standardized test scores, and because so many high schools have the same clubs, the essay is your opportunity to differentiate yourself from your competition. For this reason, writing a memorable, personal essay is particularly important to give yourself the best chance to gain admission to the school of your dreams.

The main takeaways

- DO write a memorable essay.
- DO pay attention to instructions on college websites.
- DO consider the college application as a holistic process.
- DO start preparing as soon as you can.
- DON'T assume a college doesn't have hidden essays or instructions.
- DON'T wait until the last minute.

What Is and Is Not a College Essay?

by Ren-Horng "The Hollywood Writer"

Before you can begin the college writing process, it is vital that you understand what type of essay is required. This chapter will provide you with the necessary information to write a successful essay.

This is not a five-paragraph essay

Forget what your English teachers have drilled into you about MLA structure, formality, and tone in your writing. Throw it all out. Formal writing is stiff, boring, and lacks the stamp of your own voice, and that's not by accident. MLA is designed to sound academic and impartial, which means personality is supposed to be stripped out of "formal" English writing. Therefore, in writing your college essays, MLA stiffness *must* be ignored because this type of writing squelches your voice—in essence, squelching everything that makes you unique. And uniqueness is precisely what you want to convey in your college essays. In other words, you want to write an essay that will set you apart from your peers.

This is not an SAT vocabulary test

One of the biggest mistakes I see students make is trying to jam in as many SAT words as they can into their essays to make themselves sound impressive. More often than not, people who try this tactic only end up sounding self-important (which is really annoying to college admissions counselors). No one talks like this, and this is the most obvious way to tell admissions committees that you're just putting on a show. Such an approach will just make you sound fake, and NO ONE likes fakes. Additionally, students are more likely than not to use these words incorrectly, making them look *less* instead of more intelligent.

Therefore, write with your own voice. If some difficult words are part of your daily vocabulary, it's fine to use those words as long as they sound natural. Seriously, though, don't try to cram difficult words in just to impress people. This approach is more likely to backfire.

This is not a résumé

When you submit your college application, the colleges will also receive your activity list, which contains clubs you've participated in, organizations you've led, awards you've won, and so on. Some colleges might even ask you to upload a résumé onto their application. The essay is not a place to retell admissions officers every detail of your activity list, and, no, turning all the bullet points into sentences isn't going to fool anyone. The University of California system has even gone on record to say that the "résumé essay" is the *most detested* kind of essay that they receive every year.

... So, if the essay is not these things, then what is the essay?

The essay is a place for you to either expand on something on your résumé that you want to develop much further or discuss something entirely new. Remember, the intention of the essay is to give the college admissions officers more information about *you*.

This IS about YOU

Students often complain to me, "My life is so boring! I have nothing to write about." While it may be unlikely that you've been kidnapped and found, cured cancer, or escaped a war-torn country, that doesn't mean that your story is not worth telling.

Your life experience may feel unremarkable, but don't forget that no two people have the same life experience (even identical twins!), and that with that experience comes a certain perspective of the world. Taking those points into consideration, *everyone's story is unique.*

Long story short: A story does not need to be an epic superhero tale in order to win over an admissions committee; however, it does need to show them who you are.

Furthermore, don't be too worried about trying to cater to what you *think* colleges want to read. Catering to an audience outside of yourself will only produce inauthentic writing that doesn't really show your true self. It's even possible that the colleges would prefer the authentic you over the inauthentic one who is trying to erase him/herself just to please others, so why risk it?

Sometimes it takes a little outside perspective to truly appreciate what is special about your life experiences. Seeing what stories are worth telling might be hard from your subjective point of view. However, bouncing ideas off of friends, teachers, and counselors can help open up new ways of seeing your own life. This newfound perspective can translate into fresh and exciting stories for a college admissions reader.

Stay focused

My advice is to go in the opposite direction of the résumé essay. Pick one aspect of your life that you'd like to give more attention to and expand on it. Show the reader why this story is personally significant. Ask yourself the following questions: What information about myself is missing in my application that would be best illustrated by telling a story? How does that story highlight who I am and what I value?

That being said, you don't have to expand upon an item from your résumé. Your essay topic could be on a hobby, a personal experience, or something from your daily life that you wouldn't usually think about as something to brag about. Whatever you do, make sure you put enough focus on the importance of why you picked a certain topic so your story doesn't get lost in an overwhelming flood of unfocused information.

Stay relevant

In one of my first editing meetings, a student pitched me a story about something that had happened to her when she was in third grade and asked if she could write about it. The main question to ask yourself when you reach that far back into your past is, "Does this story inform the reader of who I am today?"

If the story begins and ends in the past, I do not recommend going down that road. Who we are as third graders and who we are as high school seniors are (hopefully) radically different. A story that ends in the past cannot adequately illustrate to the readers who you are *today*. Remember, the admissions committee is looking for *who you are now* and whether you would be a good fit for their school. Only talking about what happened to you as a wee one in elementary school would not give the readers that sense.

This caveat aside, some stories that happened in the past can be good topics. If something that happened when you were a toddler continues to inform who you are today, it's possible material. However, *don't* get lost in telling the story of what happened then. Instead, focus on *who you are now* <u>because</u> of that incident.

The humble brag

Although it is important to promote yourself, you do not want to come across as arrogant. Expressions like "words cannot describe how indescribably awesome I am" will not win you any allies on the admissions committee. Of course, we want you to stand out and your application to be amazing, but how do you do this without tooting your own horn?

The answer is … show, don't tell! Don't give us adjectives to describe your character. Instead, tell us a story of your actions. As writers will tell you, *action is character*. What you do when confronted with an obstacle or a difficult choice illustrates who you are as a person. Therefore, tell the reader of an instance where you took action that also highlights the character traits that the admissions committee should know about you. If you're philanthropic, tell them about a time you volunteered. If you're a creative problem-solver, tell them about a time you got people out of a jam. Telling readers about your actions will be a much greater sales pitch of your character than adjectives alone can ever achieve.

Use vivid details

So, how do you show and not tell? Well, you must place the reader in the scene of your writing. Instead of saying that you were in a "cozy room," tell us about how comfortable the sofa was, how soft the lighting was, and how warm the fireplace was. Instead of saying that you passed by a "creepy house," tell us about the broken windows, the peeling paint, the falling shingles, the countless cobwebs, and the overgrown lawn. Relying too heavily on adjectives (and adverbs, too) to describe a scene instead of going into the details will shortchange your storytelling. If the word limit allows, provide visual descriptions so the reader can see the whole scene in the way that you experienced it. The better the picture that you paint for the reader, the more immersive, realistic, and convincing the story will be.

Again, the essay is about YOU

One of the most common pitfalls in essay writing is when a student writes about an inspirational figure. Instead of focusing on how that person has influenced him/her, the student ends up writing about that particular person. Yes, you can say that your inspiration was your mother, Albert Einstein, or Leonardo Da Vinci, but remember, ultimately, those folks are not applying to college—you are.

Yes, as young writers you may feel insecure about talking about yourself, but that's what the college essay is for. If you want to mention someone who is important to you, don't forget that you're still *the* main character of your essay. Therefore, your emphasis should focus on how *that person has influenced you.*

For instance, instead of writing about why Thomas Edison is such a great role model because he persevered even when so many of his inventions failed, write about how Thomas Edison's perseverance has inspired you to persevere against obstacles. Remember, the most important subject is YOU.

Bringing it all together

The college essay is not your typical English class essay. Instead, it is a unique, personal story about who you are today. The essay should focus on one aspect of your character that you would like the admissions committee to know about. In order to show your character and values, you should describe actions not simply use adjectives and adverbs. All in all, you should write something that is personally significant to you... a story that only you can tell.

The main takeaways

- DO write the story you *want* to tell.
- DO tell a story about who you are now.
- DO describe action instead of just using adjectives and adverbs.
- DO focus on yourself, not others.
- DON'T write like you do in English class.
- DON'T use vocabulary you don't understand.
- DON'T merely turn the bullet points of your résumé into sentences and call it an essay.

Introduction to Narrative Writing

by Ren-Horng "The Hollywood Writer"

It doesn't matter if you're planning to major in STEM or comparative literature; if you know the rules of narrative writing, then you have the ability to express to the world that great, personal story locked within you. If writing isn't a skill that comes naturally to you, don't panic. We'll guide you through the process.

Why narrative writing?

Before getting too far, I do want to clarify that *narrative writing is not the only way to write a successful college essay* (see "Introduction to Thematic Writing" and "Breaking the Rules"), but it is one of the *clearest* ways to show your personality and values. As stated in the chapter "What Is and Is Not a College Essay," stories of your own actions are much more effective and illustrative of your character than the skillful use of adjectives and adverbs. Why? Because *action is character.* Therefore, to best communicate to the admissions officers a story of your actions, you need to know the basics of storytelling and narrative writing.

Stories are about overcoming conflict or solving problems

The essence of drama—what hooks readers and never lets them go—is to see the main character overcome an obstacle or solve a problem (and hopefully triumph). The pursuit of this goal and tackling the hurdles along the way are the glue that brings together all the different aspects of a story. Without a goal or a conflict, there is no story. The words on the page just become a list of events without relevance to each other or emphasis on significance. Reading a narrative without conflict would be no different from reading a journal that details waking up in the morning, going to the bathroom, brushing one's teeth, and making and eating breakfast—boring! Such details are not usually mentioned in books, movies, or TV because such humdrum activities don't advance the character's goals or solve the problem that needs to be overcome. I'll state this rule again:

Without conflict, there is no story!

Now, this doesn't mean that the problem has to be huge. It could be something as simple as helping someone look for a job on the Internet or even fishing a bucket out from a water cellar. Either way, a good essay should tell us:

- What you wanted
- What made it difficult for you to achieve what you wanted
- How you achieved your goal (if you did)

You don't need to have an epic conflict to have an intriguing story. It just has to be intimate and show us who you are.

A good narrative has a proactive main character

What sets a good narrative apart from a bad narrative is that good narratives have proactive main characters. The story doesn't just *happen to* the main character; rather, the main character *makes the story happen*. The reactive character, whom life happens to, is not a leader and thus not appealing to colleges or to readers in general. Don't be that character.

In life as in literature, as the main character of your own story, you should not simply let the story of life happen to you. You should be the one making life happen. Tell the reader a story of how your actions made a difference, impacted a life, or inspired others. How did you take the lead? How were you a go-getter? These are the kinds of questions you should ask yourself as you decide on the story you want to tell.

As a side note, being a leader does not require you to have a title like "club president" or "committee chairperson." Besides, you probably know people who have these titles and don't do much anyway, and colleges would know this, too. The point is, these titles are for *managers*, not leaders. A manager is a person who delegates tasks, tells someone what to do because of the way power in an organization is structured. *A leader is any person who inspires others to follow in their footsteps*, regardless of whether that person has a title or an important position in an organization. In that sense, any person who does volunteer work is a leader because s/he is a role model for his/her community. If you have ever inspired people to be better versions of themselves or set an example for others to follow, then congratulations—**you are already a leader!**

A sympathetic character is aware and reflective

A narrative is not just an order of events that happens to a character on her journey to achieve her goal. What makes the story come alive are the feelings the main character has as she meets obstacles and works through them. What makes a story universal are the deeper meaning and reflection that can take the lessons of this experience and morals of the story and apply them to other situations in life.

Stories worth telling are about growth. The realization of this growth comes through reflection and the awareness of the change in perspective from before the events of the story and after. If no growth has occurred, then why was the story worth telling in the first place?

Reflection also tells the reader a great deal about the main character's (specifically your) maturity. A perspective that remains narrow and lacks proper perspective (refer to the chapter "Psst… Your Privilege Is Showing") gives off an attitude of entitlement and lack of gratitude that will only grate on the reader, leaving only negative impressions of the applicant. So much could be wrong with the world, but if you are in the position to be applying to college in the United States—and this is not meant to belittle those students who do face very real challenges in their economic conditions and family situations—chances are you are doing much better than a large population of the world that doesn't have running water, a stable government, or even food on the table. Be appreciative of what you have. Telling a story about how you had a conflict with your father because he wouldn't buy you the car you want is not a winning story. At all.

That being said, merely saying how grateful you are for having a comfortable life at home (be that in the U.S. or in the suburbs) when you see poverty in the city or a developing country is only a surface-level reflection. To get into a deeper level of reflection, get personal. What is the problem you solved? Who were the individual people you impacted? What are long-term, specific (not blanket), and self-sustaining solutions for the particular problem that you encountered? And what are you still doing or planning to do to be a part of that solution?

What comes first, the narrative or the prompt?

Whether you are applying to the UCs or through the Common Application or the Coalition, you will be given a choice of prompts to select and answer. You might find yourself looking for what might be the easiest prompt to answer and try to write accordingly.

But that's not the only option. Try writing with a story in mind first. The danger of writing to a prompt is that you might pick what's easiest and not what makes the best story and completely forget about the craft of storytelling. After all, it's an intriguing story that will hook the reader and leave a memorable impression, so write something that's good, not something that's easy.

Every story can have multiple layers of lessons that could be applied to a wide variety of prompts. After the story comes out, you can fine-tune the essay with keywords from the prompt to make sure that you

1. Answer the prompt, and
2. Highlight the lessons, values, and personal qualities that you want the admissions officers to notice.

Case study

My student D. initially showed me an essay that was essentially a résumé in prose format. It detailed some of his experience of being a Boy Scout, of the volunteer projects he had worked on, and of how he was also the captain of his high school soccer team. The essay had difficulty finding its focus, and his different activities competed for attention, resulting in the activities being shortchanged in their depth. I told him to try again.

After I had sent D. a few sample essays to read, he came up with the following for his next draft a few days later:

> At the transit home in Kathmandu, Nepal, I saw different-aged boys and girls playing with several dilapidated soccer balls. What surprised me was not the poor, worn condition of the balls, but the fact that none of the boys and girls talked to each other or played together. There were no cries of joy or exclamations to pass the ball. Each child hogged the ball and kicked it around by himself or herself. Each child has a background story and a set of experiences before coming to the transit home. As a result, they were shy and wound up. But they all had one thing in common: love for soccer.

> I decided to buy not several, but one new soccer ball. It was beautiful and everyone was captivated. But they seemed stunned and unsure when I told them to play together.

> I had served as captain for both my high school and club soccer teams, but during my two week stay after I had finished renovation every day, I became the new soccer

coach for the children at the Firefly's Children Home.

Our practices did not involve footwork, conditioning, or elaborate drills. My sessions were simple and planned with one goal in mind: to teach these children to communicate, open up, bond, and express themselves both on and off the soccer field.

Before, all the kids had one common soccer idol. Neymar of Brazil. He was adored for not only his brilliant soccer skills but also his swagger—the attitude that he could take on the opposition by himself and win.

But I introduced to these kids a new source of adoration: the German soccer team. The Germans epitomized the benefits of teamwork and communication. As the saying goes, Brazil had a megastar in Neymar, and Argentina had a superstar in Messi, but Germany had a team.

I wanted these kids to understand the power of trust and love. When they learn how to place confidence in others, in their friends, they become more confident themselves.

When I arrived, I was greeted by dull sounds of soccer balls rolling on cobblestones. When I left at the end of my two-week tenure, I left with the symphony of joyful voices crying out to each other ringing in my ears.

This is actually a pretty good start. The final product would later help get him into Dartmouth, despite his 3.7 GPA. So what did D. do right in this draft?

- He established a problem he'd like to solve (get the kids to trust each other).
- He took action (by teaching the kids soccer).
- His actions led to the kids learning the lesson he had been teaching.

What was he missing?

- Vivid detail. We still needed sensory detail of the children's home where D. volunteered.
- Stronger emotional connections. Who are these children he was teaching to play soccer?

Emotionally connect with the reader

As stated in the last bullet point, D.'s new draft did not give the reader much of an idea of whom the children he was teaching to play soccer were. Of course, with only 650 words available in the Common Application essay, D. could not introduce every kid that he interacted with on the soccer field. Therefore, D. chose one child, Rosani, to be emblematic of the transformation that the kids underwent during the course of the story.

When I read the final draft D. handed me, I felt that Rosani's presence in the essay really rounded out the story. I hope that you feel as I did that the finished essay makes for quite a moving read:

> Barefoot children in ragged clothes were playing with dilapidated soccer balls on a small strip of cobblestone at the Firefly Children's Home in Kathmandu, Nepal. When I first met them, what surprised me the most was not the poor, worn condition of the balls, but the fact that none of the boys and girls talked or played together. Each child hogged the ball. There were no enthusiastic exclamations to share. They lacked the joy of playing soccer as I had experienced it.
>
> Soccer has always been a crucial part of my identity, but my summer in Nepal allowed me to utilize soccer to convey the power of trust and family.
>
> After years of volunteering through Boy Scouts, I knew that people, especially children who have experienced trauma such as domestic violence, imprisonment, or the death of family members, have a hard time coming out of their shell. Rosani, a withdrawn twelve-year-old girl, whose mother was

imprisoned for drug possession, was always hesitant and afraid of interacting with others. However, on the soccer field, she was bold and energetic, tirelessly chasing after the ball. She and the other Nepali children all had one thing in common: love for soccer, prompting me to make an abrupt decision.

Soccer is a game of trust. As my high school team captain, I must have faith that my teammates will perform their roles. I wanted to teach Nepali kids like Rosani trust and communication to open up to the world.

In my two weeks in Nepal, I became the Firefly Children's Home's unofficial soccer coach. Rather than buying several soccer balls, I only bought one. Its beauty captivated everyone. Rosani was excited by the new ball, but she and all the children seemed stunned as to how to share it.

Our practices did not involve traditional drills. My sessions had one goal in mind: to teach these children to open up and bond with each other on and off the soccer field.

During practices, I purposely mixed the boys and girls into teams. The children had to call each other's names before passing the ball. I required at least five passes between teammates before allowing shots on the goal. During scrimmages, Rosani hogged the ball less and involved more of her teammates. By encouraging the kids to express themselves on the field, I hoped that they would gradually become comfortable playing, laughing, and connecting with each other.

Before I arrived, all the kids idolized Neymar of Brazil. They adored him not only for his brilliant soccer skills but also for his swagger and winning attitude.

I then introduced a new source of admiration: the German soccer team. The Germans epitomized teamwork and communication. It's commonly known that Brazil has a megastar in Neymar, but Germany has a team.

Over the next two weeks, I witnessed miraculous transformations. Kids who were once shy and quiet were now running energetically on the field, screaming enthusiastically. The older kids had grown into leaders not only as team captains but also as older brothers and sisters. Rosani, once shy and withdrawn, now supported her teammates and encouraged them when they made mistakes. Off the field, she matured into a mentor who reaches out to comfort younger kids traumatized by past experiences.

I wanted these kids to understand the power of trust and love. Relying on the support of others is not a weakness; it is the first step toward becoming a more confident individual. When these kids face future challenges, they will be better prepared, knowing that they have family to rely on to overcome any obstacles.

In Kathmandu, I tried to transform a group of strangers into a loving family. When I arrived, I was greeted by the dull sounds of old soccer balls rolling on cobblestones. When I departed, I left with the symphony of joyful voices crying out to each other ringing in my ears.

Rosani's presence gives the reader someone else to identify with and invites the reader to get to know one of the children whom D. impacted with his actions. Rosani became the emotional thread and heart of the story, even though D. still remained its main character. The extra detail that Rosani provided made the essay not just about a goal accomplished, but a relatable—and therefore, universal—story of a traumatized girl coming out of her shell.

Bringing it all together

Narrative writing allows you to tell stories of your actions to illustrate your character; however, the stories you pick must contain conflict, challenges, or problems to overcome and a goal to achieve to make for interesting reading. Also make sure that the story you write is the most interesting or illustrative story about you, not just one that fits the prompt.

As the main character of your story, you must show that you make life happen and not have life happen to you. Furthermore, you must show maturity, perspective, and gratitude to be likeable. To make your story more memorable, make sure you have an emotional throughline to draw in your readers and make your specific story universal.

The main takeaways

- DO use action to illustrate your character.
- DO remember that stories must contain challenges to overcome for interesting reading.
- DO show emotions, reflection, maturity, perspective, and gratitude.
- DON'T simply write for the prompt that seems easiest.
- DON'T just leave your essay at the surface level of events. Dig deep!

Introduction to Thematic Writing

by Michael "The Rising Star"

Do you have a hard time picking just one experience suitable for a prompt or find difficulty in setting up a narrative to exemplify all your hard work? Thematic essay writing might be for you. It provides an alternative way to answer prompts that do not begin with, "Tell us about a time when..." Perhaps most importantly, thematic essay writing conveys clear reflection, self-knowledge, and focus. The following chapter will address how to accomplish such a tall task.

Why thematic writing?

Although we usually reserve "themes" for literature and analysis, the significance of themes touches our personal lives as well. This is not an essay in which you will extrapolate and then, with examples, explicate a central or significant theme in a literary work. Rather, the task is simply to identify a "theme" from your life, actions, or experiences and highlight several ways that this was demonstrated, or to elaborate on and contextualize a critical observation.

Not your schoolteacher's thematic essay

We have already discussed the key differences between the English classroom "analytical" essay and the college essay, but the distinction is even more critical and even thinner in the case of the thematic college application essay.

At first glance, our description would leave the careful reader somewhat puzzled, as it appears to follow a similar structure to the five-paragraph "analytical" English essay we are so used to writing. However, this is not true. Some superficial similarities aside, they have different goals. In an essay for English class, the goal is to try to and effectively construct, explicate, and defend an argument about a literary piece. You can mimic the five-paragraph essay structure, but only in a superficial sense. The overall mood, tone, and content of a college essay is wildly different. A college application essay is a personal essay, first and foremost. The only reason we would mimic the several body paragraphs that we would use in other essays is because paragraphs exist naturally to separate ideas (the subjects of the topic sentences/body paragraphs) into a coherent, flowing explication of a more central or universal idea (the thesis).

The intro should still serve to introduce the topic, and you may even be able to point out some coherent "thesis." The real benefit of thematic writing is that you can use the structure of an essay that you are used to while employing a style that is not directly analytic.

The structural similarity basically ends there. In fact, I would encourage all of you to throw out the rigid "topic sentence/ evidence/ commentary/ repeat...concluding statement" structure that many of you are probably familiar with from school.

Differences between narrative and thematic

Ultimately, the end goal of a "themed" college application essay is roughly the same as in a narrative or other type of essay: to give a positive impression of you, the applicant, in a way that paints you as a match for a particular major, program, school, etc. As such, the types of themes or takeaways you wish for your audience to have are largely the same.

The central difference lies in the structure and the specific content of the essay. Thematic essay writing, as stated above, is a good option when the prompt is not asking you to recall a specific time or memory, but is more open-ended and subject to your decisions regarding how to present yourself.

When is thematic writing useful?

A thematic response to a prompt might be particularly helpful when the prompt asks you to demonstrate something over time, such as leadership skills, intellectual interest, etc. Instead of focusing on one narrative, you might want to highlight several distinct anecdotes or experiences you had and describe them in a shorter but nonetheless cohesive way.

Thematic writing may also be useful when you wish to give a general impression of something while still tying in multiple points. As opposed to an anecdote or story, you can more traditionally approach the process of conceptualizing for your reader by introducing it, stating your main idea, and then explaining exactly what you really mean in paragraphs.

Themes are impressions, landscapes, and feelings

The most obvious analogy to a theme in your personal life is a personality trait, and the way that we construct this impression of who you are as a person is incredibly powerful and meaningful. We can expand that concept to include topics such as interests, patterns of behavior, or even personas, to name just a few things that might be so ingrained in your life that they may as well be part of who you are. Ideas like these require illustration, but not argumentation, as said earlier. As such, we should be focusing on highlighting the actions without getting lost in wording.

REMEMBER:
- Focus on expressing yourself—do not simply anticipate what admissions officers want to hear, but focus on what makes you special. This will be the most compelling, memorable part of a thematic essay.
- Take the time to brainstorm an introduction.
- Follow structure.
- OUTLINE. This is essential for any good essay, but especially given our structured one. Because you are

reiterating your point by making repeated transitions to supporting reasoning or examples, as in both essays above, you should try to plan those out ahead of time.

Below are two sample essays that should help demonstrate the points we've outlined.

Sample Essay 1

For this Common App essay, Student 1 chose Prompt 7:

> **Share an essay on any topic of your choice. It can be one you've already written, one that responds to a different prompt, or one of your own design.**

Pay close attention to the use of structure and examples that mimics a typical 'school' essay. Pay even closer attention to the way that the student attempts to use more personal language and unique sentence structures and paragraph formatting in order to distinguish this as a thematic, personal college essay.

I'm sick of the question, "What do you want to be when you grow up?" I never give the same answers as my peers—doctor, engineer, scientist—because being studious in science or math classes never enthralled me. For me, learning has never been about reaching a particular goal. Rather, I have been inspired to learn about law and politics because of the import they have for society. I enjoyed that, in law and politics, you don't stop at the right answer—you develop and express critical thoughts and connections between varied subjects, and you eventually develop concrete perspectives on how to change or improve society.

One way I pursued a junior legal education was through mock trial, where we attended many competitions, learning about legal jargon, procedure, and argumentation. Every year, we argued a case that reflects relevant social issues, such as the unlawful use of social media or the current immigration disputes. I enjoyed mock trial because it incorporated justice into speaking. The ideological basis of law and justice are important to me because people have rights, and those rights should not be infringed upon for malicious purposes. I perceive laws as crucial tools for fighting systematic oppression and seeking justice in society. Due to my passionate effort, I took up a substantial role by helping and coaching other team members. For this, I was even elected co-president of the team.

These philosophical and social foundations of law inspired me in classes like my AP US History class, where we covered the ratification of the Constitution. I was deeply intrigued by the stubborn politics that gave way to compromise and growth over the history of the United States. I furthered my understanding of politics by joining We the People, a national competition that simulates congressional hearings. This exposed me to constitutional law, and I specialized in federalism debates, learning their contemporary relevance, especially towards issues such as regressive voting laws and sanctuary cities. My team even visited Washington D.C., giving me the opportunity to hear from Georgetown and George Mason professors, and even federal judge Royce Lamberth. In D.C., what inspired me most were not the beautiful monuments but the lectures we heard from the professors. They discussed topics relevant to today's political government, such as entertainment news' effect on political polarization and the expanding powers of the executive branch.

One question I won't forget came from Professor Mark Rozell of George Mason University, who asked us, "Who else is going to lead in this world?" This question helped me realize what I wanted to be when I "grew up." From the amalgam of my experiences learning about law and government, I feel inspired to pursue a career in civics, to hopefully one day play an influential role in building a better, more just society. One way I've enacted this vision was when, earlier this October, I organized the schedule for a voting registration drive at my school with the 18 & Uprising Group. I felt proud that I registered many new voters, encouraged those already registered to participate, and provided crucial information on ballot initiatives to those who had questions and concerns about what they perceived was a tense election cycle. To develop my education outside of school, I signed up for the Alameda County Citizens academy, where I learned about how my county is run in all sectors from the economy to criminal justice to environmental factors. I chose to participate in local, community classes and activism because I am still grasping the scope of political and legal issues, and I realized I could make a direct impact on this level. As I continue seeking to positively impact the world, for justice and for others, I am excited to discover new paths involving law and government that await my answer.

What I like about Sample 1 is that, although the student did not have the best resume or application and struggled to creatively express herself, she still effectively summarizes her views.

What would I improve? I think this essay could do with more spice, more personality, as it mostly prioritizes listing as much as possible. I would caution you to shy away from lists, as they don't do justice to expressing the student's passion.

This essay was ultimately effective, as the student had only a 3.0 GPA but was still admitted to several colleges, including the University of Missouri and the Ohio State University, both seemingly out of reach for someone with low grades and test scores. It was effective because it focused on her strengths, which in this case were her impressive list of extracurriculars and volunteering experience and her cogent understanding of the topic.

Sample Essay 2

This essay was used for several writing supplements for Student 2's application to private schools, including Johns Hopkins and the

University of Michigan. The prompts asked the student to describe an activity that they enjoy.

Indeed, I have created for myself many names—Velrand the Elvish rogue, an easily-bored artifact-seeker; Talezar of Villognia, wizard of the House of Tuorich; and my favorite character, Envar Zalmund, Ranger of the Avarian Empire, a wandering warrior who adventures with a warlock sporting a British accent and a sorcerer who lives to use the *fireball* spell (he likes explosions, you see). The warlock? My friend Patrick. That sorcerer? Mark. Our adventure? To play Dungeons & Dragons until our eyes bleed.

Indeed, I have concocted for ourselves many tales. Distinctly, I remember staying up late, chuckling to myself endlessly, writing about the latest exploits of Derrick Percival Ryginald von Rolandia III (his friends call him Reggie), the noble paladin who would constantly exclaim "JUSTICE!" during his battles with evil. But he didn't battle alone, and neither did I.

In making the world, I write for my friends, and indeed for the community of all D&D players. As I make more characters and maps, more game mechanics, and more narratives, I share them, as do they; and as we do, our world becomes livelier; the stories of its peoples become ever more connected; the cultures of its peoples become ever more real; and *we* as people become ever so slightly wiser—wiser to creating a good story, wiser to each other—for our characters each contain a piece of ourselves within.

Each character, each story about the world that we've created together, from the singular to the many, contributes to a grand narrative of both self and community—that is our game. For that is just as it is in real life; we live in the community we have created; each one story out of many, each one small piece of the grand narrative that is the world and our time.

At the end of the day, where indeed is my creativity? It is in our world and its peoples, our heroes and their battles, and in these legends of our creation that have been immortalized in the annals of our community's history.

Essay 2 might sound a bit nerdy to many of you, or even a bit pretentious to some. However, what I truly like about it is that it drips with personality. Even if the vocabulary or the esoteric nature of its content may be slightly off-putting, this student effectively sticks to his own style and sense of self. This is one benefit of thematic writing: rather than summarize or provide imagery and then follow with reflection, a writer can circumscribe an issue without unpacking every detail.

Now, what would I change? I think that this student had a tendency to get in his own head and would perhaps deliberately attempt to transcend the prompt and the occasion for his writing (college applications). It seems like he wants to opine on the subject a bit. Overall, I think he and I found a good balance for his personal style, which is the most critical thing.

The importance of personality

As indicated above, a sense of self (confidence and personality) are essential to college writing. Thematic essays are helpful because they emphasize personal description when done correctly. No matter the type of essay you are writing, it is imperative that the reader is able to connect with you. Thematic essays do this by doing the absolute best they can do to illustrate your sense of self. Without this, there is little to be gained from the reading process, and you won't make an effective or memorable impression in the admissions officer's mind.

How do we write personality? The most important thing to begin with is using the correct descriptive language. By this, I do not mean using imagery in the exact same sense as the narrative writing. Rather, <u>focus on choosing the words you would use yourself</u>. Do not emphasize or describe any one thing objectively. Do the opposite—highlight your subjective experience and interpretation of what it is you are doing.

In particular, I believe this makes thematic writing effective for writing prompts that ask you to describe. Whether it be your thoughts or an activity, giving a truly subjective—and thus irreplaceable—interpretation is what will leave the best impression. Of course, you should edit your writing to be readable and relatable, as I did with Student 2, but beginning from a personal note is key.

Bringing it all together

Theme essays and thematic writing allow the writer to provide an interpretation to the reader. This, like other types of college essays, is important to indicate the moral character of the writer. Thematic essays are engaging because they follow the basic pattern that you are used to writing, but still demand creativity and personality in order to truly get going. Do not be afraid to have a clear introduction, thesis, and sub-points in your paragraphs. However, do not rely on this formula, as the most important details are your personal descriptions and word choice. Above all, be sure to reiterate, reaffirm, and re-contextualize your singular theme.

The main takeaways

- DO write on singular, coherent points that drive the essay forward.
- DO use considerable transitions to add flexibility and flow.
- DO use word choice to manifest a sense of personality.
- DO structure, outline, and plan ahead—very key.
- DO reiterate, reaffirm, re-contextualize your singular theme throughout, doing so in a way that allows the essay to flow and progress with a compelling sense of dynamism.
- DON'T confuse "theme" with literary themes.
- DON'T focus too much on narration or narrative perspective.
- DON'T follow the exact same paragraph structure as that of a typical thematic essay.

On Imaginative Writing and the Creative Process

by Michael "The Rising Star"

Your college essays must be personal and unique to help you stand out among the tens of thousands of applicants an admissions office considers. Imagination and creativity will be your best friends to help you effectively express emotion and depth. Thus, embracing the creative process is vital to produce writing that conveys the most memorable you.

Imagine a roomful of college applications

Imagine being stuck in a stuffy room surrounded by a dozen or so people all talking very loudly and obnoxiously about how awesome and amazing and talented they are. This, at least in my book, qualifies as the stuff of nightmares and what I often imagine the job of the application reader must, at times, be like. Because if you multiply that scenario by the thousands and imagine yourself, again, this time alone in a fluorescently-lit room sitting at a desk stacked to the ceiling with college applications, the last thing you want is to listen to someone, for the twenty-seventh time that day, explain to you what an awesome and amazing and talented person they are. I think most people would want out of that room, too.

Because just for a second, I want you to imagine all the students behind those hundreds of thousands of applications. Imagine all the football players, the basketball players, the soccer players, the team captains, the ballet dancers, the violinists, the cellists, the pianists, the scholar athletes, the roboticists, the MUN delegates, the debaters, the math whizzes, the computer experts, the film buffs, the history buffs, the comic buffs, the artists, the photographers, the writers, the bookworms, the class presidents, the valedictorians. And imagine they all have dreams and visions for their future that are not too dissimilar from your own.

37

This isn't to say that you aren't unique or that you can't tell a unique story. Nor is it meant to terrify you. Quite the contrary. It is meant to kindly suggest that there is an opportunity here in your application essays to truly highlight something singular about yourself, to draw me into your world, and to make you stand out amongst the crowd, all shouting to be heard.

The question then becomes: how do *I* stand out?

"In the particular is contained the universal." - James Joyce

Uniqueness comes from particularity, and particularity comes from details. This is what you're shooting for—particularity and detail. *That* is what makes you *special*; *that* is what will make you *memorable* and hopefully differentiate you from the next applicant, who maybe has a similar background of interests. That is what you want to get down on paper, but how exactly do you do that? Fair question.

Think about your interests and passions. What is your thing? Everyone has one; everyone has *something*. Whatever it is, write about it. If anything, past experience has shown me that students tend to write stronger essays when they care and believe in what they are saying. You are being given a platform, a podium to talk about whatever you want, so use it wisely. Ask yourself: what would you want to talk about nonstop for hours, if someone were to let you?

I understand that there is a statistical likelihood that the topic you choose will be the same as someone else's. That's okay. There is still room to carve out your *own* story. This will require you to focus on the *details* behind your motivations and the *particularities* of your emotions. So maybe you're not the only person to play basketball. But what about those Air Jordans you saved up to buy or your lucky jersey you haven't washed or your team's pre-game tradition that involves a strange dance combination? Don't be afraid to be vulnerable or sentimental. Out of these details, your reader will begin to see a real person emerge.

So, where do you start?

Begin by reading the prompt and highlighting key words. The key words will be your guide.

> **Common App Prompt #1**
> **Some students have a <u>background</u>, <u>identity</u>, <u>interest</u>, or <u>talent</u> that is so <u>meaningful</u> they believe their application would be incomplete without it. If this sounds like you, then please share your story.**

Then start with a map. Brainstorm and write. Don't think, don't plan (but have a map, at the very least), and just write. Forget everything you've been taught about topic sentences, hooks, and five-paragraph essays. Once you identify the world you want to describe, start jotting down the things that make up that world. Make lists. Sketch out diagrams and ideas. Any experiences, moments, places, people, objects you want to explore in your writing, write it down. Now describe it in as much detail as possible. Think about the journalist's five W's: Who? What? Where? When? Why? Focus on sensory details. What do you see, smell, hear, touch? Or rather, what do you want your reader to see, smell, hear, touch? Remember you are inviting a reader into "your world," so you want to allow them to imagine it clearly, to visualize it, and to be a part of it. After you've felt like you've exhausted everything you can possibly say, move onto another topic, another moment, another idea.

Don't worry about making sense or about transitions—yet. Don't worry if something seems irrelevant to you. Write it down anyways because it might be important later.

Once you have written down everything—and I mean everything—print out your "essay." You now have your first draft. What next?

Trust the process

A first draft is precious. Don't share it with anyone, not yet at least. Just as you wouldn't screen a film you hadn't edited yet, you wouldn't want to show anyone your uncut, unfiltered thoughts. Now read through it with a pen or a highlighter and start circling or highlighting key words, important sentences, the most compelling anecdotes—anything that stands out as "interesting." These are the destinations on your map.

I cannot emphasize this enough to students: good writing is all about revision. Even if, after you finished your first draft, you only highlighted a couple of sentences out of a page's worth of material, that's okay. That is the job of a first draft: to identify content, and direction. The job of the next few drafts will be to find your form.

Take Student A, for instance, a basketball player. He wrote a first draft. It was what I like to call an "overview essay." It didn't focus on anything in particular, but summarized his entire four-year high school basketball career, describing how, when he started playing in freshman year, he wasn't the best player, but then he practiced really, really hard until, by the time he tried out his junior year, he made the starting line up on the varsity squad.

Why is this not good?

For one, it essentially tells the story of hard work paying off with "reward," which reflects a way of thinking that is not all that "interesting." It's okay to be proud of your achievements, but as the focal point of a personal essay, it really doesn't work. Furthermore, as an adult reader, I always feel slightly put off by such an essay, as I know that hard work sometimes *doesn't* pay off. What else did you learn/gain/understand from your hard work that was, maybe, unrelated to achievement?

For two, the essay is unspecific, thus generic. It tried to cram three years of experience into the span of 650 words. It felt like I was looking at his life from a bird's eye view, and from that distance, everyone's life tends to look kind of the same. Once you get down to the moments that make up a person's life, you start getting to where the "life" is. I didn't tell him exactly that. I told him it was essentially a missed opportunity to go into detail.

After his first draft, I asked him to read through it and identify one particular passage that he thought was the most well-written. He chose four sentences that focused on a particular night in which he sat in his car after he missed a game-winning shot and just stared up at his high school gymnasium. I agreed with him. The writing was vivid and compelling…and *particular*. So we made the decision to cut out everything else and focus on that night. I then asked him to write some new material, exploring his interiority— what was going on in his head as he sat in his car. This small moment bloomed outwards and became a vessel for his reflections not only on his missed shot, but on a season's worth of triumphs and failures, his lucky pair of sneakers, strange pre-game rituals, and the realization that basketball was about much more than basketball; it was about the accumulation of memories and experiences the sport gave him.

The bane of most young writers is early drafts. Get rid of the notion that you are going to ace this on the first try or the second one or even the third. With each pass you make in the editing process, you will remove irrelevant details, redundant ideas, clichés. Read each new iteration, look for new ideas that have come to light. Don't be afraid to go down a new path. It might take a half dozen tries, but be patient. Trust yourself and trust the process.

Thinking small

Common App Prompt #6
Describe a <u>topic, idea, or concept</u> you find so engaging that it makes you lose all track of time. Why does it <u>captivate</u> you? What or who do you turn to when you want to <u>learn</u> more?

This is usually the first mistake I see students making, believing either:

a.   they need to make their story seem bigger than it is or
b.   they don't have a big enough story to tell.

Let's take a look at an example. Student B wants to study materials science. This student has done a lot. He's taken AP Physics, been in robotics for four years, interned at labs—way too much to fit into such a short essay. After reading a first draft, I told him, "Not all of it needs to be in the essay. Think smaller." I asked him to think qualitatively, on a specific experience, perhaps the moment he first realized his interest in materials science. I asked him to write a "scene."

He wrote this:

> I first became passionate about materials science in junior year when I was in my bedroom, listening to music on my speakers. Thinking of the research I'd done at MIT on 2D materials and nanotechnology, particularly in graphene, I was laying there, and I thought if there was a way I could use graphene to make a prototype of a thermo-acoustic speaker out of this thin, flexible material.

There are obviously major flaws with just these first two sentences. It's still too expository. It still "tells" me rather than "shows" me his passion. I asked the student to cut the words "passion" and "MIT" and to focus on the emotion and excitement of building his speaker. The student ended up addressing this in his next draft:

> I put my ear to my graphene thermo-acoustic speaker prototype. Incredibly, a faithful rendition of The Blue Danube Waltz floats up to my ears. The sound feels sourceless, as if the music were playing in my head. I pull my ears away to examine other possible sources of the sound, but it is indeed the graphene film that is generating it! My graphene film! Who would have thought an unassuming 2"x2" square of what looks like Saran wrap could project such a clear melody?

Notice how much detail goes into this one passage. Rather than merely "telling" us about his interest in studying materials science, he "shows" us a picture of it, a snapshot that captures a moment of wonder and astonishment. Notice he does not name drop MIT because it's already in his activities list. Notice the details. It is not just music; it is "The Blue Danube Waltz." Notice that his motivations are not only clear but personal. He ties his interest to his chosen field by discussing his desire to design a speaker system that would allow him to listen to a "clear melody."

Now let's take a look at the second case

Take Student C, who is writing an essay about his experience as a member of FBLA. He has a first draft that is pretty dry, but he doesn't know where he should take it. There is nothing really that sticks out to him, no details or anecdotes. He thinks he has lived an uneventful life, so I sit down with him and I interrogate him. We volley back and forth for about twenty minutes, throwing out different ideas and directions for the essay. I can tell the student is getting fed up with some of my questions, but finally, the student says something and I feel myself sit up in my chair. "Before my team and I go into competitions," he says, "we all do this thing where we huddle around an orange and rub it."

"That's strange," I say. I ask a follow-up, "Why?"

"I don't know," he says. "No one knows why we rub the oranges."

All of a sudden, I felt like we had an essay. I told Student C to begin a new draft with exactly those words: "No one knows why we rubbed the oranges." It was both surprising and unsurprising how a seemingly innocuous detail like a fruit broke open his entire essay. I love this opening line partly because it is unassuming and partly because it raises several questions, both for the reader and the writer—who is rubbing oranges? Why are they rubbing oranges? What are the oranges for?—which the rest of the essay seeks to answer. Sure, you can read the oranges as a metaphor, but more importantly, the oranges are emblematic. They focus on a small, personal moment, and by the end of the essay, both reader and writer understand the significance of this "strange" tradition. And years after having read this essay, I still remember the oranges.

What do these two essays have in common?

Neither essay uses the word "passion" to describe their passion, for one. Neither essay is a support system for such "over-the-top" declarations like "I want to study business so I can build a better and brighter future with teamwork and collaboration" or "As a future engineer, I can design new products that will benefit my community." Rather, the students use specific and descriptive details to say essentially the same idea, but without all the sugar-coating.

While it is more than okay to have goals, to imagine what your future is going to look like, I encourage students to discuss the past experiences they've had that have motivated them to pursue their ambitions. For Student B, it is not just about engineering, but about engineering new sound. I can piece together that not only is this student passionate about STEM, but he also appreciates classical music. For Student C, it is not just about teamwork but about engendering tradition. It is the story of their motivations.

When you can write and describe your story with this kind of emotion and passion—without using the word "passion"—the application reader will be hard-pressed to ignore you. Do this, and you and your motivations will come off as honest and authentic, rather than as a general statement anyone can make about making the world a better place.

So what details actually matter?

This is a question every writer faces at one point or another in the writing process. My only recommendation: allow the parameters of your essay to tell you.

It's fine to cram in a ton of details into the first couple drafts of your essay, but in the end, you're going to want to pare it down to the essentials. Because it isn't just about having a ton of details, it's about having the right details in the right places. Depending on the focus, the angle you take, you will be able to automatically identify what's important to highlight. Don't get too precious about your writing. Good writers cut and good writing requires ruthlessness.

Additionally, you want to avoid stacking your essay with details about the particulars of your accomplishments and talents. Let your resume and transcripts do most of the bragging for you. You want to use the essay to find the right details to highlight.

There is a reason why William Carlos Williams' "Red Wheelbarrow" poem is one of the most remembered poems of the Modernist movement. With a simple image of a "red wheelbarrow" and "rain" and some "white chickens," Williams creates an entire world, showing us much more than just the wheelbarrow, rain, and chickens. He is also showing us the barn house, the mud, the oak tree in the front yard, the tire swing, the wicker chair on the porch, the fence line, and the alfalfa fields in the distance. It is not that "So much depends upon a red wheel barrow"; but rather, it is that the entire world he wants us to imagine depends on it.

As with the oranges, a single detail matters. Define the parameters of your essay, and identify the essential details. Give us the images that suggest the most. *Your* world depends on it.

Remember, show don't tell

This is why details are important; they allow you to show rather than tell. So rather than *telling* us you tried to screen-print t-shirts once, you can try

> "*Quick! It's going to dry,* I thought, as I slathered more blue onto the frame while simultaneously searching for an inch of clean space in my cluttered room where I could place the paint-splattered squeegee held between my teeth."

Rather than *telling* us you like to read, you can say...

> On a hazy Monday morning in Shanghai, the treehouse in my backyard whisked me off to feudal Japan, where I adventured with my little sister. In the afternoon, I transformed into an anthropomorphic mouse, solving crimes and getting lost in the wilderness of Kilimanjaro.

Rather than *telling* us you played a song called "Horse Racing" at a concert hall, you can say...

> As my fingers flew across the two strings, shifting up and down the neck of my instrument, the horses ran faster and faster, and beads of sweat began to appear on my forehead. I felt myself transported to the race tracks. The sun was bright, the air was heavy with tension, and the sound of hoofbeats on dirt echoed off the vaulted ceiling. As the race came to a close, my heart pounded, and my breath quickened with every measure. The horses were neck and neck, and my hand was just about to give out. Finally, we crossed the finish line and the sound of the last note rang throughout the hall.

Notice in all three of these examples, the author (as a character in his or her own narrative) is doing something. Make yourself do something. Take action in your essays. Even if all you're doing is sitting on a couch playing music, do it with passion and purpose. Remember: actions speak loudly.

Don't forget about your reflection

Storytelling, at least in terms of nonfiction, requires two things: action and reflection. The action engages the reader, gets me asking the most important question in narrative theory: "What happens next?" Thus, your reflection needs to answer my follow-up question: "Why did you just tell me that?"

This is where you "make meaning" out of your experience. What does this story illustrate about you and the way you see the world? How do you *now* look back on this experience? Although their approaches are different, all three passages below convey the significance of experience.

These are the last two sentences of the "horse racing" essay above:

> As the notes and melodies fill up my bedroom, every stroke of the bow, every glissando feels more meaningful. Now every time I draw the horsehair bow across the soundbox and in between the strings of my erhu, I travel back in time, through thousands of years of Chinese history and culture.

The last sentences of the "books" essay:

> Yesterday, I read books to transform my reality into dreams. Today, reading serves the radically different purpose of understanding and connecting with the world I live in. Tomorrow, I might be a poet writing down her worst fears, a creator of wildlife documentaries, a legislator arguing over education policies. Regardless, I will constantly be transforming myself through the books I have read and have yet to read and the power they have given me.

The last two sentences of the "screen-printing" essay:

> Making art, like living, is a never-ending cycle of problems and solutions, and I am infinitely grateful to Mr. Fang, who taught me how to cherish the art of failure. So with that, it was back to the drawing board.

Personally, I believe it is always better to end well than to begin well. As Robert McKee in *Adaptation.* says, "You can have flaws, problems, but wow them in the end, and you've got a hit."

You're in the endgame now

Once you've finished shaping and molding and forming the essay, make sure you're addressing the prompt. Print it out and read it over with a pen. Then try reading it out loud. Sometimes you can hear things you won't necessarily see on paper. Cut redundancies. Mark places where you stumble or pause. When you go back to "touching up" your final draft, these are the places you will need to tinker with. At this point, it would be okay to share your essay with a friend, a family member, or someone you trust. Someone with no knowledge of previous renditions of your essays may be the best judge of your work.

Bringing it all together

The goal of any piece of creative writing is to be memorable. This holds doubly true for college essays; however, the goal here is not just to be memorable, but to be memorable in a "good way." To do this, you ultimately want to convey emotion and depth, so don't be afraid to be intimate, vulnerable, or sentimental. Whatever your method is, you want to aim for detail, particularity, specificity. You want to focus on your motivation and your passion. You want to enjoy the creative process because, ultimately, that joy will rub off on your reader.

The main takeaways

- DO start early.
- DO use descriptive language and provide details.
- DO revise revise revise, and revise.
- DON'T expect perfection on the first draft.
- DON'T plan the essay.
- DON'T be afraid.

When to Ignore Popular Advice

by Helen "The Professor"

Advice from "experts" telling students to "be clever," "use unusual imagery," and "try to be the type of student *College X* wants" often leads to students' being overwhelmed and writing confusing, fake, and pretentious essays. Stop listening to those people! Really, the most important thing in writing your college essay is to be clear and *to be yourself.*

Student background

J. was a creative student who wanted to major in neuroscience in college. He had already read several books of "successful college essays," so he was trying to take as many of their suggestions as possible. In addition, he had already shown his draft essays to counselors and teachers.

The "college essay-writing experts" he had consulted told him to "be clever" and "creative" and "use unusual imagery" to "hook" the reader to leave a memorable impression. He had focused so much on others' advice that anyone reading his essay for the first time would have had no idea what he was trying to say.

By trying to follow "expert" advice from various sources and people, J. was trying to figure out what would get him into a good college instead of thinking about who he was or what he wanted to communicate. J. was not focused on revealing himself to admissions committees; he was trying too hard to market himself as the type of student that a particular college would want.

What *do* colleges want, anyway?

The problem with asking, "Is this what College X wants to see?" is that *only the college itself actually knows what it "wants" or "is looking for," and even these answers will vary from school to school and year to year and even admissions officer to admissions officer.*

This artificial approach to essay writing can lead to the kind of broken, scattered thought process that results in uneven, scattered essays.

Don't try to write what you *think* colleges want because you can never know exactly *what* a college wants. Take the example of an orchestra holding auditions: people will audition to be a first chair violinist for the prestige, but perhaps what the orchestra actually wants is a bassoon player. If you are a bassoon player trying to be a first-chair violinist, then you will be overlooked because you were trying to be someone else instead of yourself. Don't let that happen to you.

The essay must be able to stand by itself

Admissions officers only know and read the final version of an essay. They will never know the background of why an essay is written the way it is, nor does any student have the opportunity to argue her or his case of what an essay "really" means before an admissions committee. An essay must always be able to stand on its own.

This early draft of J.'s essay below shows comments given from the perspective of a reader, such as an admissions officer, who would not know any of our discussions or the intent of what J. is trying to communicate:

Past Common App Prompt #4
Describe a place or environment where you are perfectly content. What do you do or experience there, and why is it meaningful to you?

Pictures at an Exhibition

Without beats in my heart, I'd rather die. [find a better hook]

2AM—still working. I inch into the night, draft by draft, yet smile by smile.

The production software is running, its familiar bar cursor sweeping left to right, my eyes locked in on this <u>delectable prey.</u>

> Why "delectable?"

<u>*Grids of formidable knobs*</u> accompany jagged audio waves over a grey background—yet I don't mind. I am <u>*recording the* **moment**</u>.

> These word choices are not understandable to someone who doesn't know what you're talking about.

Sure, video cameras and Facebook pictures can serve as visual reminders of friends and occasions; a love letter from half a century ago may even bring tears to the eyes and nostalgia to the heart. But for me, my own music strikes my heart and revives my <u>*long lost senses.*</u> I truly live in the wonders of <u>*punching open a box*</u> and soaking in its vivid <u>*efflux*</u> of fragrance, <u>*figure*</u>, flavor, fear—to me, that is <u>*double-clicking on an old beat*</u>. I am an avid producer; the virtual studio is my refuge, my sanctuary.

> All of these are unclear and have confusing connotations. For instance, why are your senses lost? What is punching open a box?

RealBeat12.mp3.

The beat drops, and I do too, from the tour bus onto a sidewalk in Paris. My ears hear the nonchalant drum loop, but I see myself walking next to a flowing river, painted by the smooth legato of the strings. I soak in more of the beat, and the buzzing tone of the synthesizer finally reconstructs in my mind the loud hustle and bustle of the market. Once the music ends, though, I am left staring at the sidewalk—something is eerie about the layers of cobblestone around the center gutter.

> Is "layers" the right word?
> Cobblestones lying on top of other cobblestones?

The exact same sidewalk has been painted in my mind before, but by words—yes, solely black text! It was in lit class, which I'd abhorred—why were we expected to memorize such trivial junk like the structure of *sidewalks in Shakespeare's time?*

> What does "Shakespeare's time" have to do with Paris?

Now, as I see the Parisian sidewalk through my own music, the "trivial junk" *surrounds me, haunts me; wakes me up to a newfound respect for literature.*

> Are you actually in Paris? Reading about Paris? Writing music about Paris? What does any of this say about you as a student or person?

RealBeat139-1.mp3 [make more picturesque, not story]

A replenishing blue sky above, a *coughing dirt* trail below—something about this grave and dreadful beat teleports me to this *dichromatic hell.*

> While the attempt at descriptive language is definitely laudable, it

> probably won't be clear to the
> reader what you mean by a
> "coughing dirt trail" or
> "dichromatic hell."

The itch of sweat streams merging at my chin stings as I listen to
the *hard-hitting hi-hats*.

> Someone who doesn't play music
> won't understand this.

I *catch a flashback* of checking on each member of *my crew: half have
slumped off their bikes and are walking up the hill—the message "We have
to turn back" was clear. I call a water break, putting myself in their shoes.
"We can divide among us the remaining miles,"*

> Make sure to explain to the reader
> how you got from being in a studio to
> here.

I force a joke through my dry throat to raise the spirits, and
though we all know that's impossible, we take comfort in
knowing we are a team. Now I remember why I torture myself
with these new trips—to see not just my smiling face once I
conquer yet another hill, but *our* smiling faces.

RealBeat157s.mp3.

I am a student at a university for the summer. I walk up the
cement stairs of UIowa's medical building, looking into my
professor's laughing face. Swells of warmth gush to my jaw as I
listen to this beat, reinstating the joy of finally bursting out my
far-fetched musings about decoding brain waves and *helping the
blind see to a real neuroscientist*.

> Misplaced modifier: "see to a real
> neuroscientist?" Does this mean that

> the blind people are seeing
> neuroscientists?

Just a "That certainly can happen!" is enough to unleash brightness into my future—I feel useful.

RealBeat190.mp3

Outside, it's a cold, gloomy night; inside, a warm, lively heart—*the mellow tone* tells me that.

> Clarify here what mellow tone you
> are referring to.

A snapshot of my fellow quartet members at our charity performance immediately fills me with a surge of family.

> Likewise here, you'll want to
> explain to the reader which quartet
> you are referring to.

Though we received almost no applause from our *mobile* audience,

> So, clarify what you mean by
> "mobile audience."

swells of hotness gush to my jaw as we laugh, brushing off any mistakes we made and moving on to the next piece.

My friends scoff at the incongruity between my science-y self and *this other unacademic hobby.*

> Clarify which hobby you mean.

And I admit that a young neuroscientist pounding out hours in preparation for a Ph.D. would not be expected to stay up perfecting a beat.

> I'd probably say something like "whose long-term goal is to receive a PhD" since here you are applying as an undergrad.

Though my eyes and mind are already set on pursuing a career in neuroscience, nothing stops part of my heart from staying in producing beats.

> I'd clarify earlier that "producing beats" is what you mean by your hobby.

Three words can abort the serene rediscovery of my past: "NO HEEP HAHP!"

> This feels a bit out of place. It won't be clear to the reader what you are referring to here.

Seeing all those crazy drivers bumping rap music on the streets, the last thing my dad needed was a son like them. But similar to my friends who look down upon my unconventional passion, he does not understand the comfort zone that my music sets up for me. Immersed in my beats, I am truly myself: I sing, I beatbox, things I would never do in public—all my fears are eradicated in *this sanctuary*.

> Clarify what kind of sanctuary you are referring to.

My dad's frequent bans against *producing*,

> Producing beats?

however hurtful, reiterate how important my beats are to me—as the days without producing *progressed*, the more I realized how much I depended on them as a mirror to reflect my identity, a sanctuary to escape the frantic life as a [high-achieving] student.

> So, it's not clear which time period you are referring to here.

Synesthesia is part of my life. But my condition has only made life more colorful—look at how much of me is defined through the sensations I recall through music! [find better conclusion!] [In 30 years, I wish to look back at the beats I create in college and relive the exciting moments.] [In fact, its mystery is one reason that compels me to study neuroscience—the discovery of the undiscovered.]

> The mention of "synesthesia" here kind of comes from out of nowhere. I understand that you are trying to connect your producing beats to a desire to study neuroscience, but the link here doesn't feel that convincing.

What doesn't work with this essay

Like many STEM students, J. had thought that the purpose of the essay was to mention his accomplishments, so his first draft was a confusing combination of unusual word choices, hooks, and seemingly random mentions of his interest in and experience with neuroscience. With so little explanation of what he is talking about, his "Look at me! Look at my vocabulary! Look at my imagery!" statements only provide the reader with the impression that J. is maybe a good writer but more likely that he is a show-off.

Please don't do this.

Don't frustrate your reader!

While colleges certainly value creativity and originality in your essays, clarity should never be sacrificed for the sake of vocabulary. An unclear essay like the draft above not only fails to communicate your intent, but it will also frustrate and confuse the reader. *A frustrated admissions officer is not a happy admissions officer—and an unhappy admissions officer will not admit you!*

Therefore, always keep in mind the balance between creativity and clarity—doing so will help you best express yourself and ensure that what you are trying to communicate is not lost on the reader.

How we fixed this essay

Since every college essay markets a student to colleges, I asked J. about what he was trying to communicate in this essay. He told me that this essay would accompany a second one that would emphasize his lifelong interest in neuroscience. Since that second essay would focus on his interest in STEM, it became our goal in this essay to communicate his creativity and originality.

We needed J. to stand out among innumerable other STEM students who would all have long lists of accomplishments, internships, research projects, high test scores and GPAs. Once J. understood that, we worked to preserve as much of his originality and voice as possible, while clarifying what he was talking about.

J.'s list of extracurricular activities, academic record, test scores, recommendation letters, and second essay tailored for a specific major would already address his interest in neuroscience. We decided to make this essay very different, to distinguish him from the other more cookie-cutter STEM students, against whom he would be competing for admission.

Eventually, we were able to refine J.'s essay to the final version, below, which ended up saying what the student had originally intended to say but which he had not initially communicated clearly.

Past Common App Prompt #4
Describe a place or environment where you are
perfectly content. What do you do or experience
there, and why is it meaningful to you?

Some people write diaries; others take pictures. I record my life in hip-hop beats.

Even listening to Baby Mozart as a toddler, I experienced music in terms of other sensations: vision, odors, even temperatures— the slice of my life at the time I first hear a song encodes itself into the music. Whenever a song replays, the music revives the long-lost senses of that time. This odd phenomenon never struck me as "not normal" until I recently learned its name: synesthesia. But my condition has only made my life more colorful: I use this uncanny ability to see, smell, and feel music in my favorite pastime of crafting beats. Double-clicking on an old beat unlocks fragrance, figure, flavor, and feeling, making every new beat I compose one entry in a journal of my life, like a package waiting to be opened.

C:\Users\jesse\Music\Projects\RealBeat12.mp3

Jeremy's thrilled, gaping smile pops up as I listen to this track. While Jeremy's autistic affect always seemed zoned out, lost, something about my music software excited him, and though he couldn't express his emotions in words, I could still feel his delight when his body hunched over my computer screen—his eager face, my empathy. For Jeremy, and other special-needs students, making friends was hard, but that is exactly why I befriended him—he needed friends as much as anyone. Through my music, I can envision Jeremy again and revive memories of our friendship.

Next track: RealBeat109.mp3.

Something about this grave, dreadful beat teleports me to a replenishing blue sky and coughing dirt trail. Itchy sweat streams merge at my chin. I flash back to turning around and checking on each member of my mountain-biking crew. Sam and Alan slump off their bikes and trudge up the hill. Their message "We have to turn back" is clear: everyone is tired of trying to get through the zigzag, sheer equestrian paths to Castle Rock. Putting myself in their shoes, I call a water break, forcing a joke through my dry throat—"We can divide the miles we have left among us"—to raise our spirits. Though we all know that's impossible, we take comfort in knowing that we are a team. Listening to this beat, I remember why I torture myself with these trips—not just for my smiling face as I conquer another hill, but for *our* smiling faces.

Next track: RealBeat137.mp3.

A choke of room freshener, a robot picture on paper. The beat is melancholy, but I'm grateful. My English teacher Mrs. Clark points to the robot, saying that I am just like it—refusing to develop my interest in the humanities has dehumanized me. This is a foreign concept—why would an aspiring neuroscientist need to analyze literature? But sitting at that table with her, an epiphany struck me: I had been viewing my future solely as work and completely missed the rest of life. Though parents and friends advise me to retain my technical self, I set out to relearn all the literature I had previously deemed useless. I am glad that whenever this beat plays, the robot appears and reminds me of my imperfection, driving me to struggle to improve.

Hearing "stupid teenage drivers blasting trash music," my dad has developed a hatred for hip-hop. Often I come home from school, excited to produce a new beat, only to find the production software uninstalled from my computer. Like friends who scoff at my unconventional passion, he does not understand that immersed in my beats, I am truly myself; all my fears are eradicated—I sing, dance, things I would never do in public. My dad's frequent bans against my composing beats, however hurtful, reinforce how much I depend on producing music as a mirror to reflect my identity and escape the frantic life of a high-achieving student. Beats are my memory and my sanctuary.

Why this essay works

This draft is much clearer in expressing what J. wants to communicate. Without unusual phrasing or obscure references, J. gets his point across without creating confusion in the reader. At the same time, however, the newer version of the essay still contains extensive descriptive language and gives the reader a sense that the essay writer is a truly creative person (but not a show-off). Lesson learned: if you are a creative person and are passionate about creative writing, just make sure that you give your reader enough road signs throughout your essay so that the reader isn't confused and that the essay doesn't just devolve into creative writing for creativity's sake. To these ends, let's take a look at how we worked to fix J.'s essay.

We introduced his essay with his experience of synesthesia—the mixing of his senses—since what he was really trying to explain was how his unique way of perceiving the world as a result of his synesthesia was not a hindrance but an advantage. Expanding on his synesthesia gave him a depth that might surprise and intrigue the admissions officers. Then, the overall theme of music, breaking the essay into individual compositions of his and pairing each with the activity it reminded him of, emphasized his creativity while also allowing him to cover multiple other aspects of who he was as a person and student.

This improved draft provides glimpses into three separate aspects of his personality that he felt were important to communicate but that might not come out in other parts of his application:

1. His empathy, touching on his interest in community service.
2. His interest in athletics, friendships and leadership skills.
3. The fact that he was a multifaceted student, interested in learning and having more depth than a perhaps more "typical STEM student."

J. also included the actual file names posted to the internet for the beats he composed so that any interested admissions officer could listen to the music referred to in the essay. This touch, as well as his decision to include concrete details such as people's names, makes J. even more distinct and memorable. In sum, this new draft has the impact of making J. seem more outwardly focused than his original, more introspective essay.

Bringing it all together

The purpose of an essay is to show the colleges who you are and what makes you stand out from other applicants. While creativity is important in communicating your message, artistic flourishes should never get in the way of what you are trying to say. Furthermore, it's always best to be your authentic self in the voice of your essay. Admissions officers can easily see through students' attempts to cram themselves into an ill-fitting box, and doing so will only hurt your chances of gaining admission.

The main takeaways

- DO write what you think is important to express about yourself.
- DO write in your own voice.
- DO be clear and guide your reader from one idea to another to bring all the pieces of your essay together.
- NEVER assume your reader understands the context of what you are trying to say.
- DON'T write what you THINK colleges want because the colleges might want who you already ARE.
- DON'T try to use fancy vocabulary and obscure references just for their own sake; these overt linguistic tricks will only make you look like a show-off and are off-putting to a reader.
- DON'T crowd your essay with irrelevant tangents.

Telling the Right Story
by Ren-Horng "The Hollywood Writer"

Outside of your activities and academic performance, the essay is your chance to show the admissions committee who you truly are. Therefore, the story you tell is critical to the impression you make. Be sure to pick a story that puts your best foot forward.

Student background

C. was a good student, but his academic record was not especially strong. Furthermore, he was uncertain about what he wanted to study in college and had never written this type of essay before. When it came time to write an essay that required him to discuss a contribution or an experience that was important to him, he realized that had never done the type of thinking and self-examination that this kind of writing entails.

As editors, our job is to help students understand the qualities they have that would interest admissions committees. After discussing C.'s high school activities, we discovered that one of C's most positive experiences was his involvement in his high school's Robotics Club. The building of a robot in his junior year was a very memorable and important experience to C., so he decided that this would be the subject of his essay.

Original Draft

> **Prompt: Tell us about a personal quality, talent, accomplishment, contribution or experience that is important to you. What about this quality or accomplishment makes you proud and how does it relate to the person you are?**

During my junior year, I joined my school's Robotics Club. In my time in the club, I observed many interesting behaviors among my classmates.

Our process of creating the robot was mostly made up along the way. While we started with a basic idea of what we were going to do, most of the intricate workings were made and remade well after we began building the chassis. It was a messy process: the wheels had to be attached and dismantled at least six times. Creative solutions, both practical and impossible, were created all along the way.

The group's collaboration was a combination of the shared goal to build a functioning machine and like-minded thinking. The project's success was probably ensured more by the group's collaboration rather than actual knowledge or skill; after all, only 5 or 6 of us knew what we were doing at the beginning of the school year.

The community that surrounded the club was always in a cheerful mood. There was never any hostility or anger, even when we had to rebuild parts of the robot multiple times. I suspect having a plan and measurements may have helped with that problem. The group as a whole was generally motivated when there were tasks to be done, not so much when we had more people than jobs which was most of the time.

I found that without a focus, creativity was wasted on impractical ideas, but without creativity, the flow of solutions stagnated. The challenge, the leadership, and the motivation to see the robot work helped keep people on task. Although the progress was slow and messy, by the end of the day, the robot worked.

What doesn't work in this essay

Typical of early drafts that focus on activities or events, his approach was loosely chronological, with some speculation on its significance tacked on the end.

This approach is not very engaging. *If your essay looks like this, you are not done.*

The problem with this structure is that the reader spends most of the essay not knowing the essential points the student is trying to make. This structure also tends to serve the event rather than the student.

This essay was also typical of early drafts in that the student had misinterpreted the purpose of the prompt. C. understood this essay to be a description of an activity that he had enjoyed rather than a story about his own character development and understanding of himself.

The right questions to ask to improve your writing

Your essay should be less a story about "What happened?" and more a story about *"What did I learn about myself?"* and *"How did I change?"*

Although the first draft had many problems, the essay was actually very useful. It revealed many valuable qualities, skills and experiences C. simply didn't recognize about himself. After many conversations, C. saw his experience in a new light, with an eye toward what he had learned about himself, his interests, and his strengths. For example:

- What had he really liked in this experience?
- What had he done that he might like to do in the future?
- How did he feel he had contributed to this project?

Our conversations also helped him understand how a school might evaluate his experience:

- How will he get along with fellow students?
- What can he bring to the student body?
- How does he respond to challenges?

Below is the final version of the essay that we submitted.

Final Version

Since junior year, much of my time has been focused on my school's Robotics Club. Last year, our goal was to build a robot for the national For Inspiration and Recognition of Science and Technology (FIRST) Robotics Competition. The robot had to be able to fling Frisbees accurately and climb a metal ladder. It was a complicated challenge. Designing and building a robot was part of it, but we also had to learn to collaborate, create, plan, design and work together as a team.

We had to start from scratch. Because many veteran members had recently graduated or left, only five of 40 members had any first-hand experience building a robot. Our physics teacher and mentor had a hands-off philosophy; he wanted only to keep us from burning the school down or drilling holes in our hands. Furthermore, the school provided less than 25% of the $50,000 in funding that we needed to complete the project. The rest we earned from fundraisers and writing grants.

We started with a vision based on the requirements of the competition for that year, but it was a messy process and many revisions to our plan were needed along the way. Thanks to our inexperience, most of the components had to be taken off, rebuilt, adjusted and reattached during construction. The wheels, for example, had to be dismantled and reattached at least six times. Sometimes it was hard to keep everyone focused, as when some of our team members wanted to add a propeller to enable flight, even though it would likely have cut at least one of us in half just trying to test it. We did discover, however, that duct tape could solve many of our problems, and by the time we finished, at least 10% of the robot was covered with duct tape.

Two elements were essential to our success: a mix of people—of different classes, backgrounds, viewpoints, temperaments, skill sets—and a balance of creativity and focus. The mix of people made the team creative, but without focus, creativity was wasted on impractical ideas such as the flying robot. Without creativity, the flow of solutions stagnated. Leadership, and a desire to meet the challenge, helped balance the two, and kept people on task and productive.

It was great fun building the robot. Although progress was slow and the process messy, in the end, the robot worked and everyone was still friends. We had all learned a lot about building a robot, but we learned even more about working in a team, and everyone had a good time. Because of the sense of cooperation among the team members, I felt that I was really able to make a contribution. It was my first real experience working on a challenging technology project with a team, and it was such a positive one I hope I will be able to work with groups on similar projects both in college and professionally.

Why this essay works

In the final version, the essay was no longer about the Robotics Club but rather about the qualities of C. we wanted to promote:

- C.'s love of science and engineering
- Taking on tough challenges
- Collaboration

These were all in the first paragraph, and the body of the essay elucidated additional talents we had identified as important:

- Creativity
- Persistence
- Ability to *thrive* as part of a team

The story about building the robot had become a frame for the real story, which was what C. had learned from his experience. These lessons, highly valued by all academic institutions, and authentic and clearly expressed, made C. a strong candidate in his applications.

Bringing it all together

An essay is more than just a story. It is also an opportunity to show the colleges what you are made of. Therefore, it's important that the story you choose to tell enlightens the admissions committee on the most important parts of yourself that you wish to share. Don't lose focus on what your essay should be about—it's about you, what matters to you, and how experiences have shaped your worldview. Only by revealing yourself in the essay can the admissions committee know who you are, giving you your best chance of gaining admission to your dream school.

The main takeaways

- DO write about how experiences have affected or changed you.
- DO show qualities about yourself that are important to you.
- DON'T just tell a story; show us who you are.
- DON'T lose sight of what the essay is about: you, not the event.

Should I Write about Travel or Summer Camp?

by Ren-Horng "The Hollywood Writer"

In recent years, students have been volunteering in developing countries to demonstrate leadership and concern for others. Such a trip by itself will not get a student into an elite college, especially if the student misses the point of volunteering abroad. It is important for the student to internalize the lessons learned and show follow-up and continued passion for the cause for any such stories to be persuasive.

Going abroad looks good, right?

These days it seems to be in fashion to send kids on trips abroad, hoping that the right summer camp will be the magic bullet that gets kids into a good school. While giving kids eye-opening experiences into places in this world that they wouldn't have seen otherwise is good for their personal education, there's no such thing as a magic bullet when it comes to college admissions.

The problems of so many summer programs are primarily two-fold. The first is that for many students, it's a one-shot deal. Saying that your one summer digging wells in Africa changed your life isn't going to convince any admissions officer if:

1. You only did this once.
2. You never followed up on the place where you went.
3. You never followed up on the social causes that took you on the trip in the first place.

Without the follow-through—that is, further work on and exploration of whatever issue you were exposed to during the summer program—the experience will prove to be shallow and will be seen as a resume-padder, not something that was actually substantive or meaningful to you. Which brings up the second problem:

Your privilege is showing

Being able to travel or attend camp in the first place is also a matter of privilege. So many smart and good-hearted kids who come from impoverished backgrounds can't afford to fly overseas to a developing country. Admissions officers will know that it's not fair to admit someone because s/he had parents who were wealthy enough to buy a shallow experience for their student, and they'll actually be *insulted* if your essay comes across as saying that your privilege can buy you a spot in their school. So many hard-working kids could be just as qualified for admission, but their parents just don't have the resources to send their kid abroad. Colleges know this. Therefore, colleges will not fall for shallow experiences.

What was the depth of your experience?

If you have already gone or are planning to go on such a trip, own up to the experience. Follow through. Prove that the experience really did impact you, and that it wasn't just a one-time fling. Prove that you didn't just get your feet wet but that you really jumped into the water. If you participated in a program about homelessness over the summer, continue working for homeless advocacy or affordable housing after the program is over. If you participated in a microfinance program over the summer, continue working in entrepreneurship, microloans, or economics when that program is over.

Such actions not only show that you have immersed yourself in this travel or camp experience but also prove that you have dedication to the cause. Schools want people who will be the next generation's movers and shakers, so prove with your actions in following through on camps you've been to by continuing to work on social causes that your travels were affiliated with.

What about travel for travel's sake?

The risk here is not just that traveling for fun is the pursuit of the privileged but also that such an experience is not immersive. For instance, staying in four- or five-star hotels around the world is a much more insulated experience than staying in hostels with strangers from five different countries and sharing your room with them. The first experience would make for an essay about being pampered, spoiled, and isolated from real cultural experiences. The second experience could make an interesting and engaging essay about multicultural interaction. This second option would be a possible essay topic, as long as you acknowledged that such an experience was something that you were *fortunate* to have.

If you're writing about your travels, then you need to also reflect on how the travel experience has changed you. If the journey didn't or hasn't changed you at all, then there's nothing to write about. An outer journey should only be a mirror for the inner journey; it is not a substitute. Do not mistake the two!

Your inner journey

What about those who have never traveled? You can write about your inner journey—how you came to be the person that you are. Showing how you have grown up and changed and become the person you are will be *infinitely* more interesting than someone's travelogue that's just bragging about how s/he was able to ski in the Alps. The internal journey, even if you stayed in one place for most of your life, is what counts and can be incredibly compelling. Your inner journeys are what show who you are and what you're made of.

Focus on one aspect

Finally, your essay is best if you get specific. In 500-650 words you won't be able to do justice to everything that you experienced. If you try, your essay could sound general and watered-down. Instead, focus on one experience in your travels that you want to highlight. Sure, anyone could have backpacked Europe in one summer, but not everyone discovered the resulting camaraderie of networking with Key Club members in Germany. The more specific your essay gets, the more personal it becomes. That is what the admission officers want to see—who you are.

Sample Essay

The following essay by J.W. talks about her summer camp experience. She was admitted to Northwestern and Barnard and chose to matriculate to Northwestern.

> A brand-new motorcycle was parked inside Mrs. Yang's house, located in a remote village in China, symbolizing upward economic mobility and hope for her grandchildren's future. With the motorcycle, her family could get to the city easier, so her grandchildren would not have to walk two hours each way to get to school in town.

> Her improved life started with the small loan I had lent her when I was fifteen, through a non-profit organization named Timely Rain.

> Ever since that accomplishment, microfinance has become an essential part of who I am. Having grown up in China, I feel a certain kinship with these people with whom I share the same culture and language—I want to do what I can to improve their living situation. In the summer of 2013, I participated in a philanthropic microfinance summer internship in an impoverished Muslim village in Ningxia, China. After a few rounds of interviews with Mrs. Yang and her family members, my teammates and I selected her out of four candidates to receive a small loan of $500 USD. She told us that she wanted to buy a few sheep to raise and sell them later to pay for her grandchildren's schooling. We were all moved and touched by how much she values education for her grandchildren.

> This internship fueled my passion for finance because I enjoy working with numbers, coming up with different

marketing strategies, and assessing risks. I felt that I was increasing people's economic opportunities when I constructed financial statements and business plans for potential borrowers and analyzed their ability to repay loans. Completing my first, full business plan gave me a great sense of accomplishment. Coming back this year because of my interest in rural economic conditions in China, I was eager to revisit the villagers to learn more about their daily lives and financial situations. I hoped to extend Mrs. Yang's success to others.

Asking for another loan this year, Mrs. Yang planned to spend this new loan on building a new house for her extended family instead of investing it in her sheep-raising business. To pay back this loan, she would have to take out more and more loans. She would be caught in a vicious cycle from which I feared that she would not be able to extract herself. I blame myself for not noticing this issue earlier in helping Mrs. Yang make sound financial decisions. Not loaning to Mrs. Yang this year pained me, but my inability to give her more advice and assist her was even more distressing for the both of us. Our efforts to fight poverty revealed the importance of education. For me, by pursuing a higher education in the interdisciplinary field of mathematics and economics, I would be able to learn more about situations like Mrs. Yang's and provide a better solution for her. For her and her grandchildren, pursuing an education means increasing their social and economic opportunities.

Even though I now live in the States, I still have a vested interest in the well-being of people in China. This coming summer, I am returning to Ningxia to teach financial planning to the local women. With education, Mrs. Yang has hope to break away from the vicious loan cycle in the future.

Why this essay works

In this essay, J.W. demonstrates how her experience in rural China impacted her personally by showing how she cares specifically for the people she has helped and how this wasn't the only time that she has visited this village. To strengthen her case, she establishes that she and Mrs. Yang have a preexisting relationship, making her ability to help Mrs. Yang's family even more meaningful to J.W. Through this detailed illustration of her experience, J.W. reinforces her belief in how important education is for everyone and outlines her plans on following up on this experience, demonstrating her motivation and dedication.

Bringing it all together

Going to a developing country and hugging an orphan just to get into college misses the point of what colleges are looking for in prospective students. Any essay about volunteering abroad should address why you care about the issue being addressed, how volunteering has impacted you in specific ways (not just broad terms of becoming more philanthropic), and how you continue to be involved in this cause that you are passionate about OR how you will be able to apply the lessons from that experience into your life.

The main takeaways

- DO show how the experience has impacted you.
- DO follow through/up on your experience.
- DO be specific in your essay.
- DON'T write about summer camp if you only had a shallow experience.
- DON'T write about traveling that has not made an impact on you (i.e. don't write a travelogue).

Making the Epic Intimate

by Ren-Horng "The Hollywood Writer"

Students can have difficulty condensing an amazing experience into a 650- or 350- (or even fewer!) word limit. Attempting to address all aspects of an epic experience will result in a half-baked essay. Instead, students should focus on one, small aspect of an amazing experience to fully develop a story that will satisfy both the writer and the reader.

Sometimes there's just too much you want to share

Perhaps you are one of the lucky students who have had an experience of a lifetime. Maybe you have traveled to spectacular natural wonders in the Amazon, backpacked by yourself across Europe, worked with the rural poor in a developing country, or taken a road trip across the United States. The images and stories are so vivid to you that you're just bursting to tell this story.

In your eagerness to tell the admissions office about your great month-long adventure abroad or the memorable, two-week summer camp you went on last summer, you try to cram *every single thing you can* onto the page—and then you find yourself hitting up against the word limit.

Saying too much is like saying nothing at all

I had one such student, K., who went on such a two-week summer camp to alleviate rural poverty in a developing country, and this is what he wrote:

> As I stepped off the bus in Dagouyan Village in the Autonomous Ningxia Region of China, I was exposed to the

81

harsh poverty that plagued the farmers of the area. The village's houses looked to be out of the Middle Ages, shoddily constructed with dirt, bricks, and wood. Instead of concrete or asphalt roads, their pathways were paved with dirt. The grateful eyes of the villagers greeted us as we walked into the large courtyard in front of our client Madam Zhao's house. Children ran around, playing games and exchanging questions with other internship members. *This village, I thought, would be our workplace for the next week.*

> See my notes at the bottom. When you zero in on a specific incident, this whole thing may change.

To help improve the lives of the people of Dagouyan, our group of sixty or so students would assist in various jobs around the area and interview numerous residents. Our group, named Sustainable Environmental Engineering (SEE), is one of the three involved in this volunteering program. We were tasked to help dig a water cellar and fix a solar panel/wind turbine contraption. On our very first day, we created a concrete frame for the water cellar by continuously shoveling cement onto a designated area. *It was very laborious – easily making it the most difficult work I've done in my entire life.*

> This is very vague. Just saying it's laborious does not do the work justice. Don't just use the adjective. Describe how you felt, how you were sweating, if you felt dehydrated or heat exhausted.

This very task allowed me to realize the difficulties of being a farmer or a blue-collar worker, giving me far more veneration for such people. Furthermore, they barely have enough money to purchase and implement drip irrigation in their fields, since they earn on average three thousand RMB per month, which translates to around six thousand USD per year.

Thus, they do not have enough currency to obtain other necessities, such as cattle and electricity from outside sources.

As such, the village must produce its own electricity, which is where we came in. SEE helped implement multiple solar-wind generators (contraptions composed of a wind turbine and a solar panel) in order to provide a steady form of power.

Visiting the poverty-stricken area of Ningxia lit within me a *metaphorical fire of philanthropy*.

> If this is the only volunteer work you have ever done, I can't say I quite believe this. How are you following through?

I understand that China is quite a sizeable country, and that its government cannot go out of its way to care for one district in particular, but it vexes me to see how poor of a condition the citizens of Dagouyan Village are residing in. This trip has inspired me to pursue a major in environmental engineering to find new ways of creating cheaper, more efficient ways of obtaining renewable resources. I wish to allow humans to survive off the environment with minimal impact, and to contribute to the improvement of the standards of living in Ningxia and impoverished areas everywhere.

> The focus of this essay is too broad. Do not write about the program in general. Trying to write about two weeks in 500 words cannot do it justice. Furthermore, lots of kids go on summer trips to exotic places, so admissions counselors see a lot of this kind of stuff. Your central paragraph was covering so much that it looked like a laundry list of activities completed and checked off.
>
> Instead, zero in on a specific incident that happened while you were in Ningxia. Maybe it was an interaction with one person you met. Maybe it was an activity that you participated in. Maybe it was how difficult it was to shovel cement. Get super, super, super specific and build this out as a NARRATIVE, a story, a creative writing piece. Anyone can write about a two-week trip abroad, but no one has the same exact experience as you.
>
> Also, you did not specifically state why you were proud of this experience, although you hint at its importance to you.

This first draft seemed to be a step-by-step travelogue of what had happened in the trip. He recounted the bus's arrival at the site, the faces of the children he saw, the poverty in the area around him, the kinds of projects that the camp program entailed, and he concluded with saying that this two-week experience "lit within me a metaphorical fire of philanthropy," causing him to want to dedicate his time to worthy causes.

All in all, it was rather rushed and trite.

Why the broad approach doesn't work

By describing the whole trip in broad brushstrokes, K. had flattened his experience into an essay that anyone who had been on the trip could have written. Everyone on the program had been on the bus. Everyone in the program had seen the poverty of the area. Everyone had participated in the same projects in the program. Furthermore, the experience was *supposed* to help students do philanthropic work. A student whose record of volunteering that isn't too strong suddenly saying that he will dedicate his life to philanthropy will sound especially phony. While perhaps true, making the statement that just one such experience changed his life is such a cliché that it wasn't going to convince anyone.

Trying so hard to describe all the elements of the big picture had deprived K. of space to write from his own unique perspective. As a result, he was unable to use the story to let his personal qualities shine. Instead, the qualities that he should have been emphasizing were being subsumed by the monolithic entity that was the summer camp. In essence, by trying to talk about everything, he ended up talking about nothing particularly special and came up with a generic 'my trip' essay.

When K. and I sat down again, I asked him, "What problems did you solve?" "How did you show your leadership?" That's when he answered, "Well, there was this one time when someone dropped a bucket into the water cellar without tying it to a rope, so I had to rally some people together to try to fish it out."

"That's it!" I told him. "That's your story."

Narrowing the focus

You may have a grand story to tell, but without the space to write all of it down in, you will be shortchanging the reader, and more damagingly, shortchanging yourself. Instead, what you should do is find an incident from that adventure that can be emblematic of the entire journey. What was one incident that best represented the trip? How does it show something greater about yourself and showcase the qualities that you want the colleges to take notice of?

In K.'s seemingly small story about retrieving a bucket that had fallen into a water cellar, he was able to fill in all the vivid details of the experience: all the thoughts that were going through his head, all the steps that he took to coordinate and lead his teammates, and how he overcame this daunting obstacle and solved a problem. The entirety of the story was all done within the context of the philanthropy program, his participation in which already showed that he was engaged with the pressing issues of the world without being in-your-face about it.

By putting the focus of the essay on solving this one problem within a larger story, K. had much greater freedom to express the personal qualities that he wanted to emphasize to his colleges: he's a leader, a problem-solver, a team player, a globally concerned citizen of the world. What he wanted to say wasn't overwhelmed by how-tos or step-by-step explanations that would have only taken up more space instead of showcasing what he was capable of doing. In his rewrite, it was his personal qualities and how he behaves under pressure that took center stage. The following is his much more focused final draft:

> "I can't believe that someone forgot to tie the bucket to the rope before letting it go," I muttered as I poked about the water tank with a long, iron rod. I peered into the murky depths of an eight-foot-deep water tank, searching for the bucket that we desperately needed to pour cement. My peers and I despaired at the setback.
>
> Two days earlier, we—a group of high school students—had arrived in Dagouyan Village in rural China. Our plan for this trip was to provide impoverished farmers access to clean water by constructing a water cellar. We would set the foundation, cover it in cement, and then dig out a deep hole from underneath. We set the foundation in the first two days. However, on the third day, we encountered an obstacle. Pouring the cement required us to fetch water constantly for

the concrete mix. Unfortunately, one of my colleagues lost the only available bucket in the water tank.

With no tool to recover the bucket, the completion of the concrete cover would be delayed. Instead of wasting time making excuses or hurling baseless accusations at each other, we rallied to solve the problem. I immediately organized our group into a "rescue party" for the bucket. We created an impromptu hook by bending a three-foot-long metal rod into a "J" to fish out the pail. As the self-proclaimed captain, I assigned a person to poke around the cistern with a long tree branch to locate the bucket and another person to tie a rope to the rod to prevent it from falling in as well.

Perhaps it wasn't the most efficient plan, but I had to improvise. The execution took far longer than anticipated. Every time my friends' branches made a clanking sound, I maneuvered my hook to grasp the pail, but I only brought up moss. After half an hour of disheartening frustration, I finally felt the bucket weigh down my hook. I carefully and deliberately lifted the pail to the surface. Even though I organized the team, we could not have retrieved the bucket and resumed our project without everyone's combined effort.

This experience gave me the opportunity to expand on my leadership and problem-solving skills and allowed me to apply the values of teamwork and communication quickly and effectively. Any future projects will have setbacks, and teamwork will be crucial to success. I would like to return to China one day to expand on the project we completed this summer with more extensive planning and organization to ensure that the entire mission progresses smoothly. Aiding these low-income farmers is important to me because I wish to extend the opportunities I have to others. Participating in this mission is only the beginning of my long journey to make a difference in the world.

Bringing it all together

Remember, even when you have an epic story to tell and want to cram in every detail, don't. You only have 650 words to tell a complete story in the Common App—and only 350 words to do so in the University of California application! —so keep it small, keep it compelling, and keep it vivid. An emblematic moment that you can explore in depth will help you go much further in expressing yourself than an unwieldy, sprawling story ever will be able to.

The main takeaways

- DO try to focus on *only one* event or problem that you overcame.
- DO use vivid detail to place your reader in the moment.
- DO extrapolate from your actions to show your character and potential for the future.
- DON'T try to summarize everything in an epic adventure. You will shortchange yourself.
- DON'T outline daily tasks that everyone in your trip would also have done.
- DON'T say how one trip made you into a philanthropist. It's just not believable.

Making the Small Meaningful

by Ren-Horng "The Hollywood Writer"

If you are like most high school students, you may have not lived a life of epic adventures where you escaped from kidnappers, ended world hunger, and cured cancer. However, that doesn't mean that you don't have a story to tell. Even the smallest stories from your daily life have significance that can be mined for an excellent story.

Student background

My student Y. was a volunteer at his local library who told me that this experience was the only one he could think of to write for his Common App essay. For most people who chase after essay stories that are monumental and larger-than-life, this subject might seem rather ordinary, perhaps too ordinary to be worth writing about. After all, libraries are everywhere, and volunteering at one is easy to do. Without flights to book, program fees to pay, or even an exotic destination to go to, what could there be to write about?

As Y. and I discovered in this essay-writing process, plenty.

Y. is a tech-savvy teenager who knows his way around computers. Therefore, his job at the library was to be a computer docent (instead of shelving books). He would often help people unfamiliar with computers with surfing the web and printing out documents, among a variety of other tasks. Indeed, these tasks do sound humdrum and unspectacular. Had he left the essay to be merely about this daily routine, then yes, it would have been rather boring. How could an essay about volunteering at the library captivate people and let his personality shine? Given these potential pitfalls, we had to zero in on one specific aspect, one specific story of something that had happened during his time as a computer docent.

Finding drama in the smallest stories

The story he found was from the time he had helped an older man—who was recently unemployed, still needing to support his family, and not too familiar with computers—to find a job.

By introducing the man who needed help in finding a job, Y. had raised the stakes in the story. Here's why his job volunteering at the library mattered: because someone else's livelihood depended on Y.'s ability to do his job. Also, introducing the fact that the man he was helping needed to support his family really raised the stakes for Y. He was placed under even more pressure to make sure that what he did for this man worked.

Y. was able to hook the reader by introducing a conflict. Good storytelling starts with conflict and how one overcomes that obstacle. Of course, this is not the only way to write an essay, but for Y., this was the technique that worked for him. By introducing a situation with high emotional stakes to his normal routine, Y. was able to tell a compelling story.

Layering significance and weaving reflections

The next technique that Y. used to make his story more compelling was *layering*.

As I introduced before, Y. was a pretty tech-savvy kid. However, he was not just content to know a lot about computers; working with computers was also something that he aspired to do, professionally. Therefore, as he talked about working with computers and helping the man find a job by doing a job search on the internet, Y. was also able to weave in his fascination with computers and technology, as well as his admiration for tech innovators such as Steve Jobs and Bill Gates, and how people like them have improved the world and helped others through technology.

Y. took his story one step further by talking about how he felt like his work—such as helping this man find a job—was also improving the lives of others on a smaller scale. Y. then discussed how in the future he wanted to make the large-scale impact that Jobs and Gates had done by learning computer science and becoming an innovator in the field.

Even though Y. was already telling a compelling story about how his volunteering had led to him helping a man find a job, he didn't just leave the story there. Y. went above and beyond the requirements by weaving in his personal reflections and aspirations. In this way, not only did Y. use actions to tell the reader about the kind of person he is, but he also tied in reflection and future goals to expand on his motivations, inspirations, and dreams.

The final draft

By using the above techniques, Y. was able to write an essay that really helped the admissions officers understand the kind of person he is and why that made him an ideal candidate for the university of his choice. In fact, Y. was offered admission by Carnegie Mellon and Cornell, and Purdue offered him a full scholarship. The following is his final essay:

> "Excuse me?" asked an elderly library patron, who was about sixty-five years old. "Can you help me?"
>
> Being a volunteer at the Palos Verdes (PV) Peninsula library, I generally help people with saving photos from the Internet, using the printer, or accessing their email. This particular patron, however, requested me to do something completely different. He wanted me to help him find a job.
>
> "I-I'm not sure I can, but I'll try," I replied.
>
> The PV Peninsula library is not only an intellectual sanctuary but also a place where I experience the pleasure of helping others. My friends and I use the library to study, surf the web,

and finish projects, but for the past two years, however, I have volunteered at this honorable establishment as a computer docent. Here, I help others understand how to operate library technology. I choose to work in this branch of the library because technology is versatile and ever-expanding, and it connects people all over the planet. I have always venerated people who have combined technology and philanthropy, such as Bill Gates and Steve Jobs. Volunteering at the library gives me a chance to perform similar actions, though on a much smaller scale.

The mission this man had tasked me with was completely outside my field of expertise. I had no experience job hunting and was completely caught off guard by his question. Nonetheless, I assisted him to the best of my abilities. He explained to me that he was retired, but in order to feed his mother and his family, he was forced to find a job. The man was formerly a taxi driver, so I helped him look for jobs that complemented his skill set. He thought that commercial delivery suited his interests, so we combed through several pages of job listings on Google and Monster. We found a listing for FedEx. He wasn't too familiar with computers, so I helped him fill in his information on an Internet form and upload his resume. We did this again for a job opening at UPS and several more jobs for the next hour and a half. I have been amazed at how the Internet has made tasks and processes such as job hunting much faster and more convenient in the few decades that the Internet has been available to the general public. I felt like I was really making a difference in this man's life. I never thought that a task that I did every day would make such a big impact on someone.

As my shift ended, and I was about to leave, the elderly man thanked me profusely. The patron believed that my help allowed him to pick himself and his family off the ground. It was a strange, yet warm feeling to accept gratitude. The feeling of gratitude is not something I expect when I work; I complete my tasks regardless. I've helped people not familiar with new technology with tasks such as opening email accounts and printing documents. Even though the people I assist are strangers, I am still driven to help them to the best of my ability.

At the PV Peninsula library, I can help library patrons enjoy the same opportunities offered to me by the wondrous marvels of technology. With the various tasks I have at the library, I believe it is a privilege to work there. My work in helping others will not stop there. One day, I hope to be like Bill Gates or Steve Jobs and use technology to improve the lives of others on a much grander scale whether it be through improved car designs, more convenient cooking appliances, or enhanced civilian defense systems. For now, however, I can help others who also want to harness technology to improve their lives and the world by guiding their research on the internet, at the library—a place where all ideas begin.

Bringing it all together

A winning essay does not necessarily have to be about an intense, epic experience. Rather, a well-crafted, small, intimate glimpse into your life can still get you into the school of your dreams. Just remember that essays about small events still should be rich in personal significance and still have stakes that inform the reader why they should care. Fully developing these details, as well as showing your character and proof of your interests through your actions, will set you on the right track to writing your best essay.

The main takeaways

- DO find a problem to solve and hook the reader.
- DO add reflection to your story.
- DO weave your passions and future aspirations into your narrative.
- DO find a story that is thematically related to the character point or aspiration you want to highlight.
- DON'T feel obligated to concoct some grandiose story to get into college.

Focus and Perspective
by Ren-Horng "The Hollywood Writer"

Students often have a hard time focusing their essays and include information that lacks the appropriate perspective. This chapter addresses both of these issues and provides guidance on how to tell the best and most unique story about yourself.

Student background

My student L. came from a family that had gone through a divorce while he was in middle school. The impact of the divorce had negatively affected his grades, and this essay was written with the intent of partly redressing his less-than-average academic performance. At the same time, L. believed that his school's baseball team was an integral part of his life, and he wanted to discuss how important his team had been to him.

> **Prompt: Describe the world you come from - for example, your family, community or school - and tell us how your world has shaped your dreams and aspirations.**

> *For two weeks before our baseball season begins, we are pushed to our physical limits by doing non-stop pushups, crunches, and sprints every day. Every morning at 6:00, parents would drop off my teammates, who were still sleepy-eyed. I however, was wide awake and ready to go. I had driven there myself, having just gotten my driver's license.*

Seems to be off to a good start. The hook reads like the beginning of a story and provides details that show that you are there and includes aspects of your personality.

I've been the oldest male in our household since middle school, so the early morning doesn't bother me. Most school mornings, I will rise early, fix a simple breakfast for my

97

younger sister and myself, pack our lunches and then drop her off at school before me.

My sister and I live with our mother; my father lives in another state.

> The essay is losing focus. The hook starts off the essay as if it will be about team camaraderie; by this paragraph the topic has switched over to your family life.

Living in a single-parent household, we have more than the usual share of challenges.

> 50% of all marriages in the United States end in divorce. While painful for families, this is not an unusual hardship that will impress the admissions office.

To make life easier for my mother, I became the "man of the house." I learned to cook and excel at it. I would come up with my own recipes, shop for ingredients, and cook for my family. My family loves my chicken and broccoli casserole the most.

Despite the marital strife that hangs heavily over my mother, *she has taught us the importance of maintaining undying optimism and faith in our lives. She has made sure to provide us with life experiences and that they enrich our lives and make us wiser and stronger.*

> The essay's focus has shifted again, away from the team, away from being the man of the house, to Mother. Stay focused!

She has taken us to Morocco, Egypt, Turkey, and many far-flung corners of the Middle East.

> The previous paragraph states that your family has more than its share of challenges. This paragraph shows that you have the means and ability to travel, contradicting what you stated before.

It made me realize that we live in a quite fortunate part of the world and that much needs to be done for the rest.

> This is a good start for a reflection, but by itself the statement is vague and doesn't seem to be backed up by plans or action.

As a witness to my parents' failing marriage and having negotiated the treacherous waters of their relationship, I gained a lot of insights.

> Again, because divorce is so common among American marriages, talking about it will not earn you points with the admissions office.

I now understand that, even despite the best intentions, human relations sometimes fail. When people who don't get along are forced to stay together, talents and resources can be wasted. I realized the necessity for empathy and skills for people to work together.

Even though my home life lacks male camaraderie, my baseball team makes up for it. They are my second family.

> The essay's focus has shifted again, back to the baseball team. What is the story that you want to tell?

We train hard together, win together, and face defeat together. Through them, I have learned the importance of teamwork; I learned to take and give constructive criticism, I learned the importance of communication. *I learned what to do, not only for myself, but for a team and any team I will be on in the future. I learned to accept feedback and respect my fellow teammates. Without each other's respect, we wouldn't function as a team.*

> Good statement of reflection. Can you take this further?

This is the world I come from, my family and my team.

> The prompt states, "for example, your family, community or school," which means pick one, not try to cover as many as possible.

They have taught me important lessons about life: how to work with people, *how to negotiate everybody's strengths and* _weaknesses_, so we can maximize our collective potential to achieve a common goal.

> What do you mean by this? How do you negotiate strengths and weaknesses?

These lessons are vital for me, as I aspire to have a career in the business world.

> Many people forget to talk about their aspirations, so I'm glad you included this, but please talk more about this, as it seems to come out of nowhere at the end.

Focus

Remember, the essay only allows a limited number of words to illustrate you, your background, and your dreams to the admissions committee, so make sure your story provides some depth through which the reader can get to know you. This essay jumps around different stories in L.'s life instead of focusing on one specific story. As a result, the essay lacks depth. The prompt itself lists "family, school, _or_ community" (emphasis on "or") not _and_ for discussing the applicant's world, so **always be sure that you are reading the prompt carefully.**

This is not to say that successful essays have never covered a wide breadth of topics. Admittedly, some have; however, doing so is risky because such a scattered approach prevents the stories you want to tell from being fully developed in such a limited space. L. would have been better served if his essay had discussed _either_ his family or his team as his world, not both.

Perspective

Understandably, single-parent families do have more difficulties than married families; however, single-parent families and divorce are very common in the U.S., with statistics showing that 50% of all marriages in the United States end in divorce. While divorce can negatively affect a student's academic performance, there are still students who maintain good grades despite such a major disruption in their family lives. Since many families experience divorce, this is not considered an unusual challenge for students to overcome. In fact, divorce is one of the few topics that I actively *discourage* our students from writing about (the other off-limits topic being breaking up with a boyfriend or girlfriend).

In general, I actively discourage students from writing about what has gone wrong in their lives in an attempt to excuse poor academic performance. As applications are overwhelmingly full of academic statistics and numbers, the essay is one of the few places where your character is allowed to shine. Think of some personal qualities that you want to show off in your essays. What are the *best* qualities that you want the admissions officers to know about you? Don't ruin this opportunity by using it as a place for excuses, and don't ruin it further by talking about your grades when your transcript already speaks for your academic performance. If you really do think that you need to mention something that went terribly wrong, applications have an "additional information" area for you to mention this.

As for L., staying away from divorce does not mean that he cannot talk about his family. Rather, this student can sidestep the issue of divorce by focusing on his role in the family, such as how he takes care of his sister, his household responsibilities, or his cooking. His role as the man of the house can show how added responsibilities have helped him grow, shaped him into the person that he is today, and how such a background has prepared him for college and the real world. Ultimately, L. decided to focus on his team instead of his family, but focusing on his family would have also been a legitimate strategy to unify this essay.

Whom is this essay about?

Four paragraphs into the essay, L.'s focus shifts from him to his mother. While his mother is definitely the most important part of his upbringing, especially in a single-parent household, L.'s essay must ultimately be about himself. Writing too much about his mother would make the essay sound like she was the applicant instead of him.

Likewise, writing about *anyone else* in your college essay is a risky endeavor. If you are going to write about someone else for your essay, you are best served by writing about that person's influence on you:

- What have you have done because of this person's influence?
- How have you changed because you were inspired by this person's actions?

Do not write about who this person is or his or her background information. Words that do not serve to show off who *you* are best eliminated, especially when you have to keep an eye on your word count.

If L. wanted to write about how important his mother has been in his life, he could have. However, L. should not just talk about how great his mother is and what she has done. Instead, he would need to talk about *how he has applied* what he has learned from her and *give specific examples* of how those lessons have changed him.

Keep your focus

As mentioned earlier, L. eventually chose to write about his baseball team instead of his family. His mother expressed concern to me that writing about sports could be seen as generic because so many students are also athletes and that he's not a state- or national-level competitor.

When speaking broadly, topics such as sports, music, or art can seem generic. The key to making your essay truly representative of you is to *choose a specific story* or narrative that best shows the admissions officers who you are. Do not just list qualities that you have; you already have a resume that does this. Do not just talk about the baseball team in general or about the last-minute win you pulled—that's tired and done. Instead, if your focus is on team camaraderie, talk about the time you all bonded over a team dinner or a rivalry with the girls' softball team. These elements are what make a story unique and show off your personal qualities.

Dreams and aspirations

Applicants often forget to mention their dreams and aspirations in their first drafts. Even when prompts don't specifically ask for it, stating one's dreams and aspirations can be valuable because it shows that a student has life goals and will become someone who will make his or her college proud.

L. remembered that this reflection on his future plans is part of his essay, but he didn't do much to tie it into the overall structure. Perhaps you've had the thought: "I have an awesome story about when I volunteered at an orphanage, and I want to be an engineer. How do I tie the two together?"

This is not an unusual problem for students to have. A simple way to tie two seemingly divergent interests together is to think about common character traits that your story and your aspirations share. L. actually does mention this:

> how to work with people, how to negotiate everybody's strengths and weaknesses, so we can maximize our collective potential to achieve a common goal.

L. tries to tie everything together by mentioning how his past experiences have given him qualities that he can translate into his career, even though as a reader, I am not quite sure how strengths and weaknesses can be negotiated; however, no matter what career field L. chooses in life, he will need to be able to work and negotiate with people to achieve collective goals. These are the skills that he can mention when elaborating on his dreams and aspirations.

L.'s essay also ends rather abruptly. Filling out the details of how he came to decide that working in business would be his aspiration would allow the admissions committee get to know L. better as a person. For instance, he could add these words after his last sentence in the above essay:

> I saw how lower-income and working-class people in Turkey were starting their own small businesses, and how they were providing for their families so that their children could go to school and have a better future. Seeing how entrepreneurship

can improve the lives of people around the world has inspired me to study business, so that I can teach business principles to aspiring entrepreneurs everywhere to help them raise their standards of living.

What if you don't know what you want to do for the rest of your life? What if your career goals are still undecided? What if you like pottery and can't think of how to relate that to pre-med? That's OK! Write about what makes you excited in life and how lessons from such experiences can apply to other areas of your life. Besides, with so many colleges asking multiple essay questions, **not all of your essays (only one, really) even need to be related to your major.** So, what do you like to do in your free time? What are your hobbies? Your interests may have real-world applications or life lessons that will naturally grip the reader!

Getting beyond "I want to help people"

Often, when I ask students what they want to do in life or in the future, the common response I get is, "I want to help people."

That's nice, but can you be more specific?

Colleges are looking for applicants who are not only looking to improve themselves but also improve the community on a local-to-global scale. To this end, volunteering with various nonprofits and hospitals can be impressive. However, given the extracurricular activities that you've participated in so far, why did you pick the ones you did versus any other possible volunteer opportunities?

- Did you volunteer in a hospital because you want exposure to the medical field so that you can become a nurse, doctor, or pharmacist? If so, then you can say that you want to *help people recover from illness and live healthy lives.*
- Did you volunteer with the Boys' and Girls' Club because you care about children? If so, then you can say that you want to *ensure that children have positive role models to inspire them to fulfill their potential.*
- Did you volunteer with Key Club because you want to be an active member of your community? If so, then you can

say that you want to *encourage people to be proactive in improving their communities and build a sense of civic pride.*

Adding these few extra words makes your desires much more specific, gives the readers more detail into your motivations, and allows the readers to understand you better.

Bringing it all together

Essays should have a clear focus, usually through a well-developed narrative. Additionally, you will always want to distinguish yourself from the pack, so write about what is specific to you. If you feel like you don't have any impressive hobbies or experiences, then there's still time to go out and find something to do! Find out what makes you quirky and uniquely you, and write about that. Just remember to keep the essay focused and tell it from your perspective.

The main takeaways

- DO acknowledge how others have shaped who you are without letting those others take over the content of your essay.
- DO choose a topic and stick to it.
- DO remember that YOU are the star of your essay.
- DON'T be too general.
- DON'T allow the focus of your essay drift onto others, as they are not the ones applying to college.

Psst... Your Privilege is Showing

by Ren-Horng "The Hollywood Writer"

Students can unintentionally write essays that are off-putting to readers because the stories they tell make them seem arrogant, ungrateful, or reeking of excess. Safeguard yourself from making this kind of mistake by picking the right story to present yourself in the right way.

Student background

A number of years back, I was called in to give a second opinion on a Common Application essay that was meant to answer to this past version of prompt #5:

> **Discuss an accomplishment or event, formal or informal, that marked your transition from childhood to adulthood within your culture, community or family.**

(This prompt has since been modified and is now **Discuss an accomplishment, event, or realization that sparked a period of personal growth and a new understanding of yourself or others**)

The student in question, W., had approached this prompt by talking about a summer when he defied his parents summer plans for him. W. is a good person, well mannered, has great grades and is extremely intelligent. Unfortunately, his essay did not reveal any of these qualities. The editor working with W. had expressed this concern, and I agreed.

What the essay had said

The essay begins with W. discussing the classes he is taking at a community college. He then proceeds to discuss how his parents pressure him into getting in touch with his roots by studying his ethnic background's native language. He further writes about how his parents want him to go to his native country over the summer; however, he is more interested in exploring Europe. After demonstrating his defiance of his parents' wishes, W. goes into a stream-of-consciousness digression full of obscure historical and literary references jam-packed with SAT words that no one ever uses in actual conversation. Following this is an internal monologue about how he wants to learn Italian and immerse himself in the culture. Such an expression in itself is fine, but he proceeds to dismiss the Spanish classes offered in school as being "too safe" for his liking. Fortuitously, his foreign language teacher connects him with a friend of hers who owns a business in Italy. The essay ends with him arriving in Italy, having made the decision to not follow his parents' advice and to strike out on his own, ready to embark on his summer adventure.

Good intentions poorly executed

I could see that the intent of W.'s essay was to show that he could make decisions for himself and was thus "becoming an adult," but it instead read as, "My parents have enough money to send me anywhere in the world, and I spurned their gift of going to my motherland by deciding to do whatever I want instead." Furthermore, statements such as calling Spanish "too safe" give off the impression that he sounds like he's too good to study what other people study, even too good for useful languages! The name-dropping during his stream of consciousness digression makes W. sound like a braggart showing off how much he knows, and no one enjoys the company of people like that. Furthermore, the nonstop use of SAT vocabulary words makes him sound like he's trying too hard to impress. As a result, the essay reeks of desperation.

While the essay is truthfully about W.'s decision-making process, when the essay ended with him reaching Italy, I was left feeling very much dissatisfied. To me, it seemed that the most interesting part of the story was yet to come, and the story just stopped.

True, the topic was how W. was able to assert his independence from his parents, and he did so through his decision to strike out on his own, but the framing of the entire essay felt off. Frankly, I would have been much more interested in what he learned when he was finally operating on his own when he reached Italy, than the whole process of opposing what his parents thought was best for him. I feel that in writing about his stint in Italy, he could have said so much more about his personal experiences and his growth than merely making a choice that seems boring at best and ungrateful to his parents at worst. The essay did not reveal a life lesson that W. had learned, nor did it uncover any kind of truth that showed how W. had matured.

So, how do you write the right way?

These are the most important aspects of you that your essay should showcase:

- That you are likeable—no one likes arrogance in a person.
- That you are reflective and self-aware.
- That you are appreciative of the people in your life who got you this far.
- That you are a contributor to the school/local/global community.

Ideally, the way to answer the above-mentioned prompt is not to focus solely on the event. It should focus on things you've learned because of that event and what you've learned that has carried through to shape whom you are today.

Furthermore, the way you write should make people like you and want to know you in person, just from the 500-650 word document that you've submitted to them. You do not make people like you by desperately trying to impress them. That smacks of arrogance and contempt for others who you think aren't as intelligent or as fortunate to have had the experiences afforded to you. So, please,

please, please dispense with trying to force SAT words into your essays, especially since everyone knows that you would never use those words in everyday conversation. You know it, and I know it—you're not fooling anyone. Use your own honest voice. As Judy Garland once said, "Always be a first-rate version of yourself and not a second-rate version of someone else."

Then, is being privileged bad?

Don't feel bad if you are privileged. Chances are, if you're reading this, your circumstances have been fortunate enough for you to be able to think far ahead enough to plan for your future. There's no shame in that, but remember, not everyone is afforded the position that you're in. Middle-class phenomena such as having your own car, having a hot tub on a patio in the backyard, or being able to fly somewhere for vacation, are privileges that not everyone has.

Likewise, as not everyone can afford a trip abroad, it's bad form to tell the admissions officers that you didn't appreciate your parents' planning a trip for you and that you wanted to go somewhere else instead. Essays that drop hints of what good fortune that you've had in your life need to show you as *humble* and *grateful* for the opportunities that have been afforded you. Not just in essays, but in life, a little humility goes a long way in getting people to like you.

But what if I'm legitimately NOT privileged?

If you're not privileged, don't feel bad either. Maybe you've had unique challenges in your life that would open someone else's eyes, if only they could read the story of your life. Of course, this doesn't mean that you need to be homeless or have grown up in a war-torn country to have a story worth telling. For those of you shooting for the Ivy League and other particularly competitive schools, you aren't required to have gone abroad, ended wars, or cured cancer to be admitted to your dream college. A wealth of meaningful experiences can be available to you just by interacting with others in your hometown. Perhaps there's a store where you work where you meet people from all different backgrounds. Think about your deepest friendships and most meaningful activities that you've done. Maybe you've had a volunteer experience that changed your life. Maybe you're really proud of an organization that you've been a member of for a long time. Maybe you have a quirky hobby that will grab a reader's attention. These are all potential essay topics that can take you far.

Bringing it all together

A winning essay should demonstrate the best aspects of a student, and regarding privilege that would mean having perspective of how big one's problems actually are in the grand scheme of things. If one is privileged, it's best to show gratitude, understanding, and appreciation for those who have helped the student along the way. Essays that spurn those who try to help only serve to make the student look ungrateful and unpleasant. Furthermore, it's best to write in a naturalistic style where complicated words are used sparingly, and when they are used, are used correctly.

The main takeaways

- DO focus on what you have learned from an event or experience.
- DO always be yourself.
- DON'T come across arrogant and unappreciative.
- DON'T use SAT words that are not used in everyday conversations.

How to Write the "Why This School?" Essay

by John "The Environmentalist"

This chapter explores how best to approach what is perhaps the most challenging college essay to write, the "Why do you want to come to our school?" essay. There are many common pitfalls that students encounter when they write this kind of essay, so this chapter will show you what those pitfalls are and how to avoid them.

What do you actually know about the school?

This seemingly straightforward prompt perhaps poses the most trouble for high school students. However, before we even talk about how to approach this kind of essay prompt, let's back up a bit. Ask yourself: Do you know anything about the school beyond its brand? Are you attracted to the school for reasons other than its brand? Could you explain the distinct characteristics that differentiate this prestigious school from another beyond something superficial like the architectural style of its buildings? If you answered no to any or all of these, we have a problem, albeit a very common one that many students applying to top colleges face.

You're applying to Harvard because, well, it's Harvard. And you're applying to Stanford because, duh, it's Stanford. Unfortunately, Harvard already knows it's great, and Stanford does too. Merely telling them in your essay what they already know won't cut it. And speaking in generalizations about a school—its beautiful campus, its top-notch facilities and professors—won't cut it either. So your task as a student, before you even get to writing your essays, should be to narrow down your school list to schools you are drawn to for very *specific* reasons that you can articulate from the heart. And this last part is key: *from the heart*. If you are writing sincerely about

113

real reasons you are drawn to the school beyond simply its prestige, your essay will be not only stronger but will also necessarily be more engaging and readable.

Specifics over prestige

Now, it is virtually impossible to fully separate the brand recognition of the school from the school itself; I'd be lying if I said I hadn't created my own personal college list based in part on brand and prestige, but these very much were not the only reasons. Ultimately I narrowed down my list of schools to those I could envision myself thriving at, based on very specific qualities of each school I was drawn to. In the process of getting more specific, some prestigious schools I had originally had on my list got the axe, and this is fine. Don't cling on to a school on your list merely because of its prestige; if fancy school X has to go because you can't come up with any compelling reasons to go there, then take it off the list. This approach will only work to your advantage when it comes time to write the "Why this school?" essays.

So, when writing the "Why this school?" essay, the general rule of thumb is the more specific the better, and the more personal the better—thus, not just that the school has wonderful classes, but rather, here are the specific classes I am excited about and why; not just that the campus is pleasant, but rather, here is an aspect of the campus culture that really appeals to me, and why. Treat giving reasons as to why you are applying to a school as an opportunity to show what your unique qualities are and why they will mesh well with the unique qualities of the school. In other words, don't try to force yourself into the school by telling them how amazing they are; rather, show them how you and the school are an ideal match, that both you and the school stand to gain from your acceptance to the school.

How you tell your reasons is still important

This all being said, even if you are specific in your essay, you can still run into the trap of simply listing aspects of the school you are drawn to. You do need to still make sure that the essay is engaging and gives the reader reason to keep reading. Thus you will have to get creative in terms of how you craft the essay. One approach is to picture yourself on campus on a typical day. What would you be doing? What would you experience? What would you see? Pondering and exploring the answers to these questions can help you generate the kind of descriptive language and imagery that can still make for an engaging essay.

To give you an idea of how the more specific but descriptive approach to this prompt can be accomplished successfully, let's first look at an example of a weaker, less specific and personal essay and then compare it with a stronger, more specific and personal one.

Example essay 1

I looked in the mailbox and there lay an unexpected letter. "It's a package from X University…" I was astounded. One of the most prestigious schools in the nation had written a letter asking me to apply to their school.

> The weakness here is that the essay immediately turns to the school's prestige, something the school already knows about itself.

Prior to receiving the letter, a counselor had recommended that I apply to X, but at the time, I didn't have the confidence to do so; I didn't think I had a chance. To my surprise, my friends also agreed with the counselor and suggested I apply. I thought, "My counselor was encouraging me to apply. X was encouraging me to apply. Some of my friends are encouraging me to apply." The only one holding me back was myself.

So I made the leap and told myself I could do this.

115

> The best approach with this kind of essay is to show resolve and determination; unfortunately, this portion shows hesitancy. Even if you did hesitate, they don't need to know this. In fact, less is sometimes more with the college essay; they don't need to know the WHOLE story, just the parts that attest to the quality of your character.

I had long known about X's engaged student body, and its merging of academic and practical endeavors.

> This topic sentence falls into the overly general trap. It is a statement that could be made about numerous schools in the country.

Now that I was on board,

> Don't include the part of the story where you weren't on board. Start at the point when you were already on board.

I started to see myself immersed within this dynamic world. Amidst the backdrop of the beautiful, serene campus

> Between "dynamic world" and "beautiful, serene campus" you've got two glaring generalizations in a row.

I pictured myself working with the X Robotics Club (I am a current FIRST student) and taking our work to the next level.

> This part actually gets closer to the level of specificity you want in this kind of essay; however, it doesn't go far enough. What kind of project? What kind of work? With whom?

I saw myself pursuing research (maybe on my idea for an aerodynamic exoskeleton) within one of its centers and institutes,

> Which center? Which institute? Is this the kind of project you could actually work on within that institute? It would have been better to clarify.

and applying for an internship to take my classroom knowledge and apply it to the real world.

> Many schools provide possibilities for internships. So how would this school provide the most ideal internship opportunities? It is not clear in this essay how.

Ultimately, I took my self-doubt, transformed it into confidence, and decided to pursue a dream: X University.

> While this concluding sentence does attempt to bring it home, so to speak, you could unfortunately put in the name of virtually any college or university after the colon. The sentence needs to be made more specific so that only one school could be put at the end.

Getting specific

So, all of this begs the question: How do I find out about specific aspects of the school that I might be drawn to? There is oftentimes nothing more valuable when it comes to learning specifics about a school than visiting. However, let's be clear by what I mean by "visiting": a visit in which you are able to see what it's like to actually be a student at that school. This means doing more than just going on a campus tour. Many smaller colleges have programs in which they will pair you up with a current student, so that you can go to classes with the student, eat in the dining hall, and stay overnight in the dorms. You can ask students questions about their experiences at the school, potentially talk to some professors, have an on-campus interview. After your visit you will have first-hand, detailed knowledge of the school that you can use for your "Why this school?" essay.

Unfortunately, many larger universities don't offer overnight stays to potential students, so gaining an inside look at these schools is trickier. One possibility is to stay with a friend who is a year or two older than you who is already going to a school you are interested in. Another possibility is to see if the school offers informational interviews with someone who works in the admissions office. Absent these options, you will have to take a different approach: Do you know any alumni from the school you are interested in whom you could talk to? If not, your best and perhaps only bet is to do good old-fashioned research—online, and by way of books on colleges. The best books on colleges provide longer testimonials from current and past students, which can give you deeper insight into what going to the school is actually like. Keep in mind, however, that this is a self-selecting group of students, as those with gripes about the school probably would not be selected to write a chapter for such a book, so the reviews these students give will all be pretty glowing.

When it comes to online research, you can find out quite a bit about a school—as far as course offerings, research opportunities, student clubs, and professors and their academic focuses—from its website. However, when it comes to questions like campus culture and atmosphere (e.g., Is it a party school? Is it a politically active school? Do students basically just study and do nothing else?), you will have to do more digging, as no school's website is going to advertise that students at their school primarily love to party and that studying comes second. Certain websites such as *www.unigo.com* can be helpful for finding better answers to these questions, as they contain reviews of schools by current and past students. Although, keep in mind that with such websites, the more prestigious the school, the more the student reviews tend to be 100% glowing, as oftentimes students at these schools are eager to broadcast to the world how they are at Harvard and are loving it and too bad you can't be as happy and lucky as I (am). So, you might have to put on your critical thinking hat and sift through some of the chaff to get to the wheat.

Okay, so you've done your homework, narrowed down your list, and you know where you want to go. Let's now take a look at an example of a "Why this school?" essay in which the student really excelled and ultimately saw success.

Example essay 2

As an innocent middle-school student, I had aspirations to play college basketball. However, those dreams quickly faded with the start of high school and a more realistic outlook. Then, my high school coach showed me an email from the School X basketball coach, and suddenly I had new dreams. But basketball was just the beginning. I soon found in School X the intellectual diversity I craved.

> The student starts out by showing sincere excitement for being involved in multiple and specific aspects of the campus community.

In the summers of 2014 and 2015, I attended the Girls in Science Day, and Basketball Camp at School X, where I listened to keynote speaker Y and learned about her work in plate tectonics. She discussed a program in development that would be able to warn of impending earthquakes and accurately report their magnitudes.

> The student goes on to start supporting what she means by "intellectual diversity" through first-hand knowledge of the school and a specific professor and her work.

I realized that at School X I would be able to work with a plethora of innovative faculty members like Professor Y who are in the vanguard of their fields and could help fuel my curiosity and passion for science.

Aside from faculty, I also met alumni and current School X student-athletes; their tours and anecdotes of life at School X I found inspiring. They led me through group houses on campus where the walls were strewn with cartoons and murals, displaying the talent and diverse, quirky minds that exist at the school. I saw the opportunity School X could provide for me to find my niche and be comfortable in an open-minded world where I can grow and thrive with others both like and unlike me.

> Through the student's descriptions of what she saw and what resonated with her at the school we get a sense of a part of who she is - that she needs to be somewhere open-minded, and that she is thrives amidst diversity, two qualities found at this particular school.

In addition, School X's core curriculum provides an interdisciplinary foundation for research in STEM, allowing me to explore different fields and apply them to my major of interest, while also becoming well-rounded in obtaining effective communication skills essential to leadership in any field. It is this flexible, interdisciplinary approach to STEM education that sets School X apart and is all the more reason why I am drawn to the school. To further round out my education, the various learning initiatives, such as the X Program, will prepare me to become an engaged student of the world, where I can broaden my views through community activism. My aspirations to become a computer scientist started with more experienced people reaching out to me, and School X's diverse extracurricular opportunities will give me the chance to do the same, to help the community grow and learn along with me.

> The student provides a specific example of how the school's particular approach to academics is unique and then complements it with a discussion of another

program the school offers, in this case, one that is focused on community activism, the mention of which gives us further insight into the student and her character.

Ultimately, my biggest source of external motivation has always been the positive, intelligent yet open-minded people I surround myself with. I know that at School X there will not be a shortage of these people. From my visits, I noticed the unmistakable camaraderie and intimacy that endures among the students, as different groups passing by always seemed to know one another. It is evident that in a small school like School X there is a helpful and stimulating atmosphere where people study a variety of courses and have a range of unique interests. All of this will help me expand my own interests and intellect to become the person I aspire to be.

The benefits of her first-hand knowledge of the school truly shine through at this point in the essay: she saw what it was like to be a student there, and a specific aspect of life there—the camaraderie and intimacy—she knew she would thrive from, as she needs to surround herself with inspiring people in order to learn and grow. Ultimately, we get the sense that this student has really done her homework and made an informed decision, that this school would be an ideal match for her, and that she would be an ideal match for it.

Bringing it all together

The name of the game with this kind of essay is to be specific, as specific as possible, and to show how you are an ideal match for the school. If it turns out that you really don't have a good reason for applying to the school other than for its prestige, it might be time to nix the school from your list and find only those that you are truly excited about going to for very specific reasons. When possible, it's always helpful to visit a school so you can get a first-hand take on what it's like to be a student there.

The main takeaways

- DO your homework on the school.
- DO be as specific as possible in your essay.
- DO match yourself and your interests to schools that welcome students who have your interests and ambitions.
- DON'T be generic in terms of why you are drawn to the school.
- DON'T just list off aspects of the school you are interested in.
- DON'T tell the schools what they already know (e.g., that they have top-notch professors, give students a world-class education, and are all around amazing).

Breaking the Rules
by Ren-Horng "The Hollywood Writer"

The advice we give in this book are general guidelines on how to write essays, but these guidelines can have exceptions. The most important lesson is that you write an essay that best reflects you, not just one that follows the rules to a T.

If you've made it this far, congratulations!

Now you know the basics of college essay writing. The chapters provided in this book are not meant to be a strict, paint-by-numbers framework but rather a guide to help you reveal your best and most interesting you. As the essay is ultimately your creation, what advice you choose to accept or reject ultimately is your decision. However, should you choose to break the rules we've presented to you, know why you're doing so and how to do so correctly, so the readers can follow your story and still remain engaged. To these ends, let's look at a relevant case study.

Student background

Q. is a young woman and STEM student who produced an essay that does not follow many of the rules that we have prescribed in this book. With this different approach, her editor helped her express herself in a way that was best suited to her, and this essay got her admitted to both Caltech and MIT. The following is her essay reproduced, which answered the 2014-2015 Common Application prompt #4: **Describe a place or environment where you are perfectly content. What do you do or experience there, and why is it meaningful to you?**

> Survival guides line the bookshelves, backpacks are stuffed to the brim with vacuum-sealed biscuits and glow-sticks, and athletic bandages are stowed in boxes under a big first-aid sign. No, I'm not in the local CVS or survival gear store; I'm

in my room. It all started when I was a three-year-old living in Taipei. I was sleeping soundly in my bed and didn't even notice that the building was suddenly shaking violently. "It's a big one!" my dad yelled from his room upstairs while my mom clutched my arm and dragged me across the living room, which was rearranging itself as the sofa hurled into the wall. Frantically rushing down twenty flights of stairs in my slippers as plaster hailed down on us, I didn't understand much of what was going on, but I knew we were in danger. Though we were lucky enough to get out in time, not everyone was, and many were injured.

My fear and trauma that stemmed from the 921 earthquake were the impetus for my interest in collecting first-aid and survival items - I wanted to be prepared for any emergency. Since 2009, I have lived in San Diego, and my room is my lab, the place where I experiment using the new Swedish flint, examine the latest type of pain-free Neosporin, and peruse over the most recent official survival guide issued to the U.S. military. It's where, after reading about how to obtain clean water, I proved to myself if distilling groundwater through boiling, collecting the steam, and then letting it revert to water really works (it does!). My room is also my family's triage center where I am eager to treat wounds whenever anyone gets hurt and finish up with an Angry Birds or Batman Band-Aid from my vast collection.

Having personal space to tinker with survival items and create emergency kits is meaningful to me because this hobby allows me to satisfy my curious nature. Considering that I still live in a region that experiences major earthquakes—and brush fires—I like the peace of mind of being prepared and having the knowledge to help others should the need arise. During the recent San Diego wildfires, for example, I made sure that my house had a good water supply, mapped an escape route from the second floor in case the stairs were engulfed in flames, and disposed of arid weeds and twigs that could easily ignite. I helped out my neighbors, too. It's in my room where I also started to examine how items in science kits work. Learning how to build an automatic light switch and analyzing DNA, I found that my interest in science also progressed at school. This led to extracurricular activities at the local science center and internships where I gained invaluable experience in lab work. Fiddling in my room is how I first discovered that I want to have a career in biology, specifically in medicine, perhaps—big surprise—as an ER doctor (though more recently, I also became interested in cancer research after serving two internships).

Most of my friends and classmates see biology and chemistry as required classes that exist to make their lives harder, so they don't understand why I voluntarily conduct science experiments in addition to school assignments. They call me a nerd, which I don't like, because I'm not a tedious person who just sits at my desk and studies all day. The truth is, I have fun filtering particles out of liquids and dissolving impurities in water. Exploring new topics in science also helps me learn course material more readily. I am really grateful for my room, where I don't have to listen to anyone deride me and can play with science in peace!

How does this essay break the rules?

It's non-narrative

Q's essay is not telling a traditional story with the structure of beginning, middle, end, or a goal and the conflict to get there.

- Why does it work?

Despite not having a story structure, this piece is *still not a résumé essay* because it doesn't go on about her achievements and awards. Rather, Q.'s essay weaves together *snippets of various aspects of her life*. Flow of ideas is still important for the readability of this essay, for disconnected ideas and poor mechanics would jar the reader out of the story and draw too much negative attention to itself.

It covers a wide breadth

Generally, we advise students to go narrow and deep to fully express one aspect of their personalities. Here, Q. has provided a wide scope of her interests and background instead.

- Why does it work?

Even though Q. doesn't have room to fully elaborate on the various aspects of her life that she is introducing, she is still *detailed*. She doesn't just say that she makes things and does experiments in her home lab; rather, she is "distilling groundwater by boiling, collecting the steam, and then letting it revert to water" and "learning to build an automatic light switch and analyzing DNA." All these detailed snippets provide the realism necessary for an essay of such breadth to come alive.

It starts in the past

I generally advise students not to tell stories about life events that occurred before high school. After all, a person changes a great deal during high school. That being the case, a story that takes place when the student was a toddler or in elementary school may not be considered relevant to who the student is now.

- Why does it work?

Q.'s story may start in the past, but its effects continue into the present. The earthquake is what makes her into someone who is always prepared, just in case of an emergency. This story of her past still affects who she is today. Had this story about the earthquake merely ended in the past without the discussion of any lingering effects, then of course the story would not be relevant to who she is today and would not be worthy of inclusion in this essay.

It has an obvious setting

When thinking of a place that people feel comfortable, the first choice people jump to will most often be their rooms. As such, someone's first thought may be that such a choice may be "too easy" or "unoriginal."

- Why does it work?

For a less interesting person, I do believe that this setting would not have worked. The reason this setting did work is because this essay and setting truly illustrates who Q. is. For a moment, don't worry too much about if an idea is original. While that is certainly a factor, most likely any "original" ideas you may have had already been attempted by another writer. What makes an essay shine is if it can truly reveal who you are. When you can show your truest self, your essay will by default become unique because there is no other person who is just like you.

Remember what an essay is supposed to do

An essay, while it should be well written, is not meant to be critiqued as a piece of literature. Admissions committees will not spend hours analyzing your word choice, metaphors, or unique turns of phrases. Unless you give the reader something memorable to impress them with, you will probably get ten to twenty minutes on your writing. As such, your goal is to reveal yourself as clearly and as best you can and leave a lasting, positive impression. In other words, show that you are exactly the kind of student that your dream school is looking for.

Bringing it all together

Because an essay is all about showing your best self, achieving this goal is far more important than concentrating on the styles of flashy story structures, metaphors, or turns of phrases. What is most important is that you showcase you in the most effective way you can while being as detailed, vivid, and relevant as possible, even if it means not strictly following all of the guidelines presented in this book.

The main takeaways

- DO express yourself clearly and effectively in your essays.
- DO use vivid imagery and details to color your story.
- DO tie in any stories from the past with who you are today.
- DON'T feel bound to rules if you feel they get in the way of expressing yourself.

The University of California Application

by John "The Environmentalist"

This chapter will explore recent changes to the UC essay format and then go in-depth into both how you approach the somewhat challenging length of only 350 words per essay and how you put together a package of essays that is compelling and effectively reflects who you are.

The UC's move from two essays to four

In 2016, the University of California announced that it would be switching from an application in which every applicant wrote two essays on the same two topics to one in which students would have eight essay prompt options and would pick four to respond to. Additionally, whereas the previous essay format had a combined word limit of 1000, the new essays would be capped at 350 words apiece. This move made it more possible for students to give more comprehensive pictures of who they are, and this possibility is precisely why the UC admissions officers chose to instate the change. Additionally, the move suggests that the admissions officers are trying to place greater emphasis on the less quantifiable aspects of a student's application and profile, and to value the student's lived experiences. In fact, we have seen many students with less-than-perfect grades and test scores but who have written outstanding and meaningful essays do quite well in the UC admissions process, getting into top UCs such as Berkeley, UCLA, and UCSD. This is not to say that you should disregard your grades and test scores, but if they aren't perfect, don't despair. Essays full of passion, honesty, and verve can help push your application to the top of the pile.

Which essays do you choose?

So, your first task is going to be figuring out which prompts to actually write essays for. Your best strategy is to first go through each prompt and brainstorm as many ideas as possible for each. For some of the prompts, you might have zero ideas, but as with any brainstorm, sometimes the best ideas will come to you days after your initial brain-wracking idea session. So, stick with the brainstorming for more than just an hour on one day. Brainstorm a bit; leave it for a while (days even); then sit down and brainstorm some more; repeat. Additionally, take the approach that all ideas are valid in a brainstorm. In other words, get every idea down on paper, and then you can go through and pick your strongest ideas.

To those ends, you will want to favor those essay ideas that focus on activities and endeavors that you have spent the most time on and are the most passionate about. These can include extracurricular and academic endeavors but may also include other activities outside of or independent from school that you have both devoted considerable time to and have learned from. Representatives from UC Admissions have consistently stated that they will be frustrated if you have indicated in your application that you have devoted countless hours to a particular activity but then you don't write anything about that activity in an essay. If you do choose to write about an academic subject, it is important that you write about what you have done within the subject above and beyond mere in-class work and assigned homework. In other words, have you done research of your own, creative writing of your own, gone to a camp that focuses on the subject? As such, you won't fall into the trap of just writing about how you like the subject a lot and have done your homework just like every other student.

When it comes to ultimately deciding which essays to choose, you'll want to think about how to create a package of essays that is focused but well-rounded. Like a good album by your favorite band, your collection of essays should all very much be quintessentially *you* but show different facets and sides of that you. In other words, you don't want to be one-note, but you also don't want to be so all over the place so as to have no singular voice or perspective. If you stick to writing about what you care about and have had the most experience with, you should accomplish this goal with little problem. Make sure, however, that you don't write about the same experience for multiple essays.

What about recycling essays from another application, say a Common App essay or a supplemental essay for another school?

While you can pull this off, you will need to proceed with care and caution. Namely, you need to make sure it is clear in each UC essay that you are responding to the prompt. You don't need to be so clear that you repeat the language of the prompt (i.e., prompt: What is your favorite subject and why? You: "My favorite subject is biology because…"), but don't have the content of the essay be so vaguely related to the prompt that the admissions officer starts to suspect that you just recycled the essay from another application. Long story short, pick your four prompts based on compelling content you can write about, not because you want to take the path of least resistance. If it turns out that after you have selected your prompts that you could use some bits and pieces from a non-UC essay, that is fine, but again, make sure that that isn't obvious.

Nuts and bolts

Now let's get down to some nuts-and-bolts tips on how to actually write the UC essay. The first quirk of the UC essays you have to deal with on a practical level is the length. Many students feel quite daunted by the small amount of space and feel like they won't be able to say everything they want to say. And this is true, you won't. This being said, to start, it is much more important that you get down on paper what you really want to say and then work on trimming the essay back. This approach will prove much easier in the long run than simultaneously crafting the essay and trying to be mindful of the word limit. When it does come time to do some trimming, ask yourself: Will my reader feel like they are missing information if I take this part out? Is this longer description I have written fully necessary for capturing the essence of an experience I've had, or could it be shortened and still create the same or a similar effect? If the answer is "No" to either or both of these, that part of the essay can most likely be pared back.

When it comes to essay structure, there are multiple approaches you could take, and in fact, varying the structure from essay to essay is advantageous, as it will ensure a reading experience that is fresh, engaging, and intriguing. Do not feel obligated to follow a standard intro-body-conclusion structure; in fact, you should never write a summary-style conclusion in a college essay, as it is simply a waste of space and says so little about you and your personality (beyond the fact that you are... boring). Instead, consider mixing things up a bit. To these ends, let's take a look at essays whose structures are all somewhat different but that still effectively answer the prompt and tell a meaningful story. These essays are in response to UC Prompt 7:

What have you done to make your school or community a better place?

Leading up to the distribution of the January school newspaper sophomore year, I investigated a story about the administration's cover-up of a wrestling coach's relationship with a student. However, after the article was published, something did not sit right with me. Around campus, I found students catapulting vulgar comments towards school faculty—comments that strayed from the contents of the article. Shocked and disheartened, I realized that the truth had morphed into a venomous wedge, driving itself deeply between the student body and our school. The public had come to prioritize criticism over connection, and controversy over community.

In the first paragraph of this essay, the student effectively gives background on an event and provides just the right amount of descriptive detail without falling into the trap of overdoing it and describing EVERY sight, sound, and smell she experienced. Notice how she does not include any sort of formal thesis statement in this paragraph; instead, she implicitly hints to the reader that there was a problem that she wanted to solve.

> I was immediately driven by a deep desire to take action—to facilitate healthier conversations about the world we live in. Calling up a few international friends I had met at a business program earlier that summer, I eagerly shared my ideas. From there, our journey with Quark Magazine began.

Here we see the student outline how she planned on solving the problem. Notice, however, that she does not simply say, "So, then I decided to do x," a phrase that says so little about one's character. Instead, she both tells us what she did and more about herself by saying, "I was immediately driven by a deep desire to take action— to facilitate healthier conversations about the world we live in." From her words we can glean that the student is driven, motivated to effect change, and values healthy dialogue.

> As a founding team from Canada and both US coasts, we set out to shape a narrative that could celebrate STEM, English, and our communities with others globally. As I now edit the fascinating articles submitted by our international writers, I know we are creating a medium that does more than thrive off of controversy. By addressing everything from the repercussions of Adderall drug abuse in high schools, to the translation of the research behind the 2017 Nobel Prize into layman's terms, we are encouraging healthy dialogues about both the ugliness and beauty of our world through the voice of this younger generation.

In the interest of space, the student could not go into a play-by-play of the whole process of setting up the magazine, nor would this approach have been engaging for the reader. Instead, she briefly outlines what the goals of the publication were and then focuses more on specific articles and topics the publication had covered thus far. We know from reading the paragraph that the publication is up and running and that its creators are realizing a vision for change.

> Having been a writer invested in a story of scandal, I understand the importance of exposing truths to the public. But I also believe that I can use my words and actions to turn the conversation into one not about "us versus them," but simply about "us," thus promoting more constructive responses even to cases of controversy. In the future, there will always be more scandals to be uncovered, more issues to be wrestled with, and more dialogues to be sparked. I know that I can make a difference in that plot, one story at a time.

The student leaves about a third of the essay to reflection and conclusion. This is an ideal amount, as UC Admissions will want to know not just about what happened and but also about how the event or experience has shaped you and your thinking since. Implicitly, this student is saying that as a result of her experiences and reflection, she's moved away from pursuing writing articles just for the sake of stirring up controversy and has taken a different approach to writing. In other words, she's describing how she's changed and suggests a new direction she will be going in.

Now, let's take a look at an essay that takes a slightly different approach.

> There's a moment of silence as I show the next slide of my presentation. On the screen, there's an image of a young boy with dark-spotted blotchy skin and a rib cage protruding out. The atmosphere of the room changes, and I automatically feel in the air that my peers seem unsettled by the image.

This essay takes a much more narrative approach right off the bat. What is key here is that the writer continues with the narrative approach in the next paragraph. Too often, students will put in three sentences of narrative or two lines of dialogue as an easy attention-getter, only to shift back to a much more straightforward style for the rest of the essay. If you are going to go the narrative route, you need to follow through with it for more than just a few sentences and make it integral and necessary to the experience of the essay. In this case, the story is a vehicle for the writer to demonstrate her passion for and commitment to a cause.

> I introduce Xiao-Ming, one of the many children I met on my volunteer trip to a rural Chinese village this summer, and recount some of my personal experiences with him: drawing murals together, playing ball, and teaching him English words. I still vividly remember Xiao-Ming's tight grip, a representation of how much he could crave, but not reach. For the rest of that day's presentation, I cover the many serious public health issues affecting that village. I describe how the villagers are forced to drink from the murky water of the Yellow River and eat scarce sustenance due to the drought. I stress how there are no toilets and only one doctor in an unequipped clinic for the entire area.

Here, the writer continues with the narrative but goes deeper to show what specifically she has done to go above and beyond and really try to effect change. As such, the writer doesn't fall into the trap of telling a tragic story simply to tug at the reader's heartstrings while not demonstrating any true commitment to the problem she is working on solving.

> My summer trip has changed my view on many things. I believe that by hosting these weekly presentations and meetings as part of my newly founded Public Health Club at Miramonte High School, I am also opening my peers' eyes. They are largely affluent students, and I want to help change their mindset about the world by revealing the struggles many still face today. I hope that with this knowledge, more people will take the initiative to spread awareness of the problem and fight this battle with me. So far, we as a club have taken wide strides toward tackling public health issues by conducting outreach events for the homeless, helping out at food banks,

and hosting public health publicity events in our community. Ultimately, I want to reach an ever-broader audience and inspire more people to act.

Notice here how the reflection begins midway through the essay, thereby maintaining the right balance between narrative and reflection. Here, she begins writing about how the experience of traveling to the Chinese village has changed her and her path in life. She supports what she is saying with specific examples from her efforts. At the end, she talks about how she wants to expand her work to affect a broader swath of people.

> What I have done is a tiny step. But someday, I hope that my own and more importantly my friends' passion on this issue and what we decide to do after college will change the future of a boy like Xiao-Ming.

In the last paragraph, the writer continues with the idea of expanding the scope of her social-change endeavors while adding in a little humility so as not to give the impression that she believes she is the savior of the world. Colleges like to admit students who are passionate and committed yet aren't convinced that they know what's best in every regard. In other words, they want students who are eager not simply to pursue what they love but also to learn. Otherwise, what would the point of more schooling be?

What style should I be using for the essays?

Now, there is some confusion as to whether you should write a narrative-style essay at all for the UCs. In fact, we have heard conflicting responses from many an admissions officer. Some prefer the uber-straightforward style; some don't. So, what do you do? Well, the takeaway should be to find your own voice and style that best represent who you are. If you are a writer at heart, show it in your essays. If you fancy yourself more of a straightforward, down-to-business person, then your essays can show that as well. That being said, don't bore the reader. You still need to tell somewhat of a story and avoid merely writing the essay version of a resume. Thus, as a general rule of thumb, no matter who you are, vary the structures and styles of your essays enough so that they don't feel like the same essay four times.

Example essay set

In fact, let's look at a set of essays that really accomplish this goal well. This particular student, L., ended up gaining admission to Berkeley, and Riverside with a full scholarship. Her essays achieve that sometimes elusive goal of being at once singular on their own but cohesive as a group. In reading through the essays, notice how she varies the style and structure of each essay so that it doesn't feel as though you are reading the essay four times. Notice too that she very much does not adhere to a three-paragraph, intro-body-conclusion structure, yet she still manages to write essays that are easy to follow and feel unified.

> **Prompt 1: Describe an example of your leadership experience in which you have positively influenced others, helped resolve disputes, or contributed to group efforts over time.**

> "You don't belong here," my mind whispered. A quick look around revealed a band room filled with confident, experienced seniors. In stark contrast, I was only a junior and new to band leadership. Wanting to fit in, I contrived to project an image of poise and authority. This image distanced me from my section, the flutes, but I believed that time would close the gap.

> Since I didn't have a 6th period, I volunteered to rehearse with the freshman flute players during their band class. I spoke only to give corrections and instructions, and as a result, the freshmen were as silent as stone. Understandably so. The atmosphere was suffocating in its rigidness.

So it was all the more unexpected when one day I cracked a pun. Hours upon hours of awkwardness had accumulated until I was ready to burst. I needed to try something different. Out of sheer randomness, I loudly made a pun during one rehearsal and jerked my head down into a double chin. Immediately, the ice was broken. A bubble of laughter rose from the freshmen for the first time. They burst into chatter.

Everything changed after that day. The freshmen, having seen that I was not just a stern upperclassman, opened up to the rest of the section, and we became more harmonious and productive as a result. The band directors praised us, noting the difference from previous flute sections.

That day, I discovered that true leadership and vulnerability were inextricably linked. My idolization of the idea of a leader had prevented me from progressing. Letting go of this allowed me to forge connections and, surprisingly, earned me more respect. Vulnerability, which indicates both sincerity and trust, is essential to impacting and inspiring others. Without it, leadership is just an act built on a façade.

Today, I continue to strive to be someone the flute section can admire, not fear. We are almost siblings to each other, and as my years in marching band come to a close, I can conclude that my proudest accomplishment has been uniting my section through a leadership of authenticity.

Notice in the following essay that L. does write about music again; however, she is writing about it in a different way. In the previous essay, music merely played a backdrop for her larger discussion and exploration of leadership and what it means to her. In the following essay, she focuses on piano and more so on the craft of it and how she has learned to personalize the endeavor.

Prompt 2: Every person has a creative side, and it can be expressed in many ways: problem solving, original and innovative thinking, and artistically, to name a few. Describe how you express your creative side.

With loose sheet music littering the ground, my teacher, Monica, and I pore over possible flute repertoire for upcoming competitions. After prolonged deliberation, I settle on Alphonse Duvernoy's Concertino Op. 45, a French piece brimming with color and dramatic runs. Monica gives an abridged rendition, and I go home confident I will be able to replicate her playing soon.

Every day, I practice the concertino diligently, moving my fingers on the keys of my flute like a typist taps on a keyboard: precisely. However, the notes sound as lifeless and dull as if I were beating them with a cane. So I lighten up. I use less air. Still no improvement. Now, I'm straining my throat, trying to force notes out. For months this cycle continues: identify an issue, fix, repeat.

When I finally ask Monica for advice, she smiles like she has always known. "Don't think of the piece as something you have to accomplish. It's not just about doing the right thing at the right time. Play it again, and this time, sing it in your head the way you wish it sounded, with your interpretation," she says. To my amazement, my internal portrayal begins to seep into my playing. The concertino comes to life, overflowing with vitality. I earn a Command Performance, the highest ranking, at the CMEA Solo and Ensemble competition that year.

From this experience, I have come to see music as a wholly organic phenomenon. Merely going through the motions of playing an instrument can only be called imitation, because technique and replication alone are not enough to make a piece my own. The secret to music, and its purpose, is the expression of an individual's voice. This secret has taught me to be bold in expressing myself, because I cannot produce anything of value if all I do is copy others. To make my mark, I must bring what no one else can. Playing the flute has shown me the significance of incorporating my individuality into my pursuits, and I am confident that, going forward, this will be the foundation of my success.

In the next essay, the student shifts gears and reflects on a family hardship that has deeply affected her. Notice, however, that instead of dwelling on the hardship alone, she really makes the bulk of the essay about personal discovery and growth, which is a recurring theme throughout her essays. Recall that colleges are really looking to admit students who have shown a demonstrated depth of character, and L. truly shows this depth through all four essays.

Prompt 5: Describe the most significant challenge you have faced and the steps you have taken to overcome this challenge. How has this challenge affected your academic achievement?

October 2012: my Second Aunt passes from lung cancer. Afterwards, I, a sheltered child of twelve, suddenly assume caregiver responsibilities for my devastated mother. My father works 9:00 a.m. to 9:00 p.m. to support our family. Out of necessity, I become the older me that my mother needs.

To lessen my mother's worries, I take on extra chores, ask for little, and am her perfect child: I keep my grades and smile up, my voice and complaints down; I drag her to doctors' appointments, nag her to eat, spoon-feed her, tuck her in to endless "naps." Every day, I clumsily juggle two lives as caregiver and student, trying to ward off whispers of anxiety. Eventually, I reach the edge. I sleep only six hours nightly, and ten pounds have vanished. Exhausted on all fronts, I wonder how I will possibly go on. I wish for anything, anything at all, to magically change my circumstances.

But hoping for something to rescue me inevitably proves pointless. Nothing changes, and I realize I am the only person who can steer myself towards a future I want. This is the grim determination that sees me through the darkest times. I pick myself up and throw my energy back into caring for my mother. When I finally hear her humming Chinese lullabies again, I know all my efforts have been worth it.

In times of difficulty, when larger events are beyond my control, my response matters more than my circumstances. This attitude of self-determination I have applied to not only my personal life but also my academic one. Often I tell myself that, whether it is a calculus test, crucial in-class essay, or complicated chemical equation, no challenge is insurmountable as long as I decide to persevere. I could choose to cling to self-pity or grief, but by moving forward, I learn and mature. I grow. Hardships are unavoidable occurrences, but I am now better equipped to deal with them and to seize opportunities invisible to others. I will take both as they come, and run towards the future I shape.

Finally, L. takes a very different turn and writes an essay in which dialogue is a central and running feature throughout the essay. Yet instead of following a simple structure of dialogue then reflection, she weaves the two approaches together to create a nuanced and meaningful essay that doesn't sink into cliches.

Prompt 7: What have you done to make your school or community a better place?

The Tenderloin.

What calls to mind a chunk of meat for most people is also the poorest neighborhood in San Francisco. This is where I met Temperance.

Last summer, our youth group made its way to St. Anthony's Dining Room, a soup kitchen in the Tenderloin. During our shift, I spotted a woman with dirty-blonde dreads in a ponytail and hot pink highlights crying. I had hoped to avoid the homeless, but I heard myself say,

"Excuse me, ma'am, are you alright? Do you need someone to talk to?"

She sniffled. "Yeah. That would be so nice."

She spent the next half hour pouring out the story of her life, a long downward spiral that began with drug addiction. While I was not surprised by her addiction, what she said next startled me: she had bachelor's degrees in both biology and psychology and had been working towards a master's. I myself had seriously considered majoring in those subjects. I suddenly remembered all the times I had skirted around the homeless in wide arcs, avoiding eye contact, because of the assumption that they were all merely drunks or mentally ill, with no life story or hopes or dreams of their own. Was it possible that we were so similar?

But how could I have made such harsh judgments so quickly?

"What's your name?" I ask her.

After a pause, she replied,

"Temperance."

I sat down to listen to her, clasping her hands in mine. Temperance did need food, but what she truly craved, few soup kitchens could give: human connection. Reviled as the very lowest of society, she nevertheless shared this need for emotional fulfillment with every other person alive, and rejection hurt her just as much as it does us. Ultimately, superficial appearances and labels mean nothing. What else could explain our similarities?

I see many more Temperances now than I ever did before. They're on street corners, at my school, and they're all like me. They've helped me embrace others and be mindful of my judgments and their struggles, stories we all carry. The humanity inside everyone.

This essay closes in a way verging on poetic and leaves the reader with the sense that L. is adept with language, a keen observer, and wants us to look inside ourselves and think about our own preconceptions of the homeless and others in general. It is the ultimate way to end the set of essays, as it leaves the reader with something to think about and ponder over. In other words, the overall effect is that the essays are memorable, and, as a result, L. was too. So it's little surprise that Berkeley wanted her, and that Riverside wanted to offer her a full ride. She showed that she had a depth of character, a curiosity for the world, and a keen desire to learn and grow—all qualities that colleges look for in those they want to admit.

Bringing it all together

Ultimately, you will want to pick four essays that will give your readers the most complete and multifaceted picture of who you are. Make sure to avoid telling the same story twice, and always ask yourself, "What will the reader learn about me through this essay? Will they learn anything new, or will it just be a repeat?" When crafting each UC essay, try not to get hung up on length right away and just write what you want to say. It is much easier to go back and cut out unnecessary bits and pieces than it is to try and write well while also being mindful of length.

The main takeaways

- DO pick four essays that give the most complete picture of who you are.
- DO be engaging and descriptive, even though the UC essays are short.
- DO leave enough room for a thorough reflection.
- DON'T tell the same story twice.
- DON'T use the exact same style for each essay.
- DON'T write about things that many students already do, such as studying hard for a test.

The Common Application: An Overview

by Matthew "The Idealist"

The Common Application, as its name states, is a common, online application platform for over 750 colleges that makes it easy for students to apply to several colleges at once. This chapter will provide an overview of the Common Application, as you should have a basic understanding of the application that will be unavoidable in your college application journey.

What is the Common Application?

The Common Application is the most widely used college application platform and for good reason. It offers applications for hundreds of colleges, and chances are that you are going to be using this platform. The Common Application allows you to apply to up to 20 colleges, which should be more than plenty for any young, budding academic.

What makes the Common App the most common app?

For starters, the sheer number of schools that are Common Application members makes it tempting for students to fill out one application and just be done, instead of searching out school-specific applications that take extra effort to fill in information that you would already be filling out on the Common Application anyway. In this case, the student benefits from ease of access and reduction of effort needed to fill out an online form. On the other hand, the universities also benefit from being a Common Application member because making their school easier to apply to means that they receive more applications and can reject more applicants, increasing their selectivity ranking.

Furthermore, the Common Application has a stylized, easy-to-use layout. In contrast, I have had many students in the past complain about the other applications' user-interface, particularly the difficulty of being unable to add colleges or move onto the next page of an application until all the checkboxes have been checked. With the Common Application, this isn't as much a problem, and a student can skip around and fill out the parts of an application easiest to fill first. If you plan on applying to 15 or more colleges outside the UC system, then the Common Application is going to be one of your best friends.

Additionally, the list of colleges to choose from on the Common Application is extensive, ranging from the top-tier Ivy Leagues to the more obscure state schools and private liberal arts schools. Essentially, the Common Application has something for everyone.

The benefits of the Common Application:

- It is user-friendly.
- It has the best/most variety of colleges to choose from.
- One application → Up to 20 colleges.

Application features

Common App

This tab, the actual "common" part of your application, asks for a significant amount of information and will require the most time to fill out. It is important that you leave yourself enough time to go through it thoroughly because this is the application that will get sent out to each of the colleges on your list. The tab breaks down into seven categories: profile, family, education, testing, activities, writing, and courses & grades, which will be explained as follows:

1. *Profile* - basic personal information, such as your name, birthdate, address, contact, demographics, geography, language, and country of citizenship.

2. *Family* - basic information about your family, in particular your mother and father, their occupations and level of education.

3. *Education* - all details relating to your high school education and academics, such as your high school, any transfers between schools, your GPA, academic honors, and future career interests.

4. *Testing* - self-report standardized testing results, as well as tests to be taken (note: you will also be required to send in your official SAT/ACT test reports separately)*

5. *Activities* - up to 10 extracurriculars you have been involved in throughout high school, including anything such as sports, community service, school clubs, internships, part-time jobs, to religion, artwork, and music**

6. *Writing* - answer 1 of 7 prompts in a 650-word personal essay (more details below)***

7. *Courses & Grades* - enter in your grades for all your classes from freshman to junior years (note: not all colleges will require this section).

Since most schools don't require you to report all your test scores, only input your strongest testing results, unless specified to do otherwise.

**For the Activities section, you will be asked to enter a description of the organization and the position you held (50 characters), as well as a description of the activity itself (150 characters). For the description of the activity, you do not have to write in full sentences. It is important, however, that you cover your role, what the organization/team/club did/has done, any achievements gained, not just a general description of the club or activity. (Example: I led the varsity soccer team to the finals and won first place → led varsity soccer; won first place). Additionally, you will need to provide your level of involvement (hours/week, weeks/year). This section tends to be very time-consuming, so it is a good idea to get started early and maybe have a résumé/CV on hand for reference.*

***It is highly recommended that for all the writing requirements (including the personal essay, activity descriptions, and supplement essays) that you write them in a separate Google or Word document and copy and paste it in once you have finished. Since the formatting can get jarred a bit when cutting and pasting, we recommend not indenting in the original document and just skipping a line to indicate a paragraph break.*

Dashboard

The Dashboard provides a quick overview of the schools you wish to apply to. Generally, it tells you what the individual requirements are for each of your schools, specifically writing requirements and writing supplements. It also provides the deadline for each of your schools' applications. **However, do not rely on this page alone to tell you what your school's individual requirements are.** For example, Cornell's application will say that it does not have a writing supplement until you pick a major, which then unlocks a "hidden" 650-word essay. Rice will only tell you on its *website* that those who want to do interviews must turn their application in on December 12; those looking only at the Common Application page will only see the January 1 deadline. Parsons has an extra "Parsons Challenge" only on its website and not on the Common Application, and the University of Michigan's Ross School of Business has an extra portfolio that is also not explicitly stated on the Common Application.

College Search

In order to add a college to your dashboard, go to the College Search tab at the top of the page and type in your desired college. If you are uncertain of the colleges you want to apply to, you can narrow down your search by U.S. state, country, writing and/or Standardized Test requirements, deadline, and so on. You have a maximum of 20 colleges that you can add onto your Common Application account.

My Colleges

Along with the Common App application, you will be required to fill out a supplemental application for each college. These supplemental applications can be found in the My Colleges tab of the Common App and are college-specific. The application includes information such as degree interests, additional activities, preferred start term, preferred residence, and writing supplements. However, the requirements for each college are different. The writing supplements are sometimes located in different sub-tabs, so you might have to go searching for them. Additionally, the writing supplements are different for every school and cover a broad range of topics, so be prepared.

Here you will also sign a FERPA waiver and invite your recommenders. It is highly recommended that you waive your right to your recommenders' letters so that colleges will know that your recommenders have been honest in the letters that they have written to the school.

The Common App personal essay

The Common App requires you to write one 250-650-word personal essay. This essay will be sent out to almost every college you apply to. While this might seem easier than writing four UC essays, it can be deceptively difficult. While the UC essays provide you with four chances to best represent yourself, here, you only get one shot to showcase to an admissions officer who you are. Therefore, since you only get one essay here, it is vital you choose a prompt and a topic you can respond to at length and one that you feel best reflects you, your personality, and your strengths.

Can you recycle a UC essay? It depends. Look through the list of Common App prompts and see if there is one that fits your UC essays. There is a chance that none of your UC essays will be a good fit or that you might have a better topic for one of the Common App prompts that you have not yet written. Also, keep in mind the possibility that you could recycle some of your UC essays for the Common App supplemental essays.

If you do decide to use one of your UC essays and expand on it for the Common App personal essay, keep in mind that there is a big word count difference between the two. While the minimum word count for the Common App is 250 words, that doesn't necessarily mean you should write the bare minimum.

Sure, concision is an important aspect of college essays. However, I also believe it is important that you be thorough, providing enough details for an admissions officer to get a good sense of who you are as a person. As you draft, revise, and edit your essay, make sure you are detailed without being redundant or overly wordy. Having said that, it is important you choose a topic that is fascinating to you—so fascinating, in fact, that you could talk someone's ear off about it.

A quick word about Common Application supplements

The Common App essay supplements cover a broad range of topics, from extracurricular activities to favorite academic subjects, to important social issues, historical moments, favorite books/movies, your chosen major, and your personal values. There are also more "light-hearted" questions that ask you to write a letter to your future roommate or describe your desired superpower. However, the most common essay prompt is probably the "Why This College" question, which will require you to do significant research about the college. That prompt is already addressed in a chapter devoted to that topic.

Here are some more example questions you are likely to come across:

1. How do you see yourself contributing to the diversity of the campus community?
2. Write about a person, event, or experience that has helped you define your values or changed how you approach the world.
3. What aspect of the college's program, community, or campus environment attract your interest?
4. How has your background influenced the problems you want to solve?
5. How have your interests and related experiences influenced your choice of major?
6. Please tell us how you have spent the last two summers.
7. Please elaborate on one of your extracurricular activities or work experiences.

For these college supplements, it is important that you:

- Not repeat aspects of your Common App personal essay.
- Do specific research about the college you are applying to.
- Tell a brief anecdote that characterizes you and your values and then explain how the college would be a good fit for you and what you stand for.

The Common App prompts

1. **Some students have a background, identity, interest, or talent that is so meaningful they believe their application would be incomplete without it. If this sounds like you, then please share your story.**

   Things to Consider: What about your history, personality, hobbies, or accomplishments sets you apart from your peers? How do you define yourself? How do the people who are closest to you define you? What have you achieved that has been integral in molding your character and ambitions? What is a specific experience you've had that demonstrates your personality and character?

2. **The lessons we take from obstacles we encounter can be fundamental to later success. Recount a time when you faced a challenge, setback, or failure. How did it affect you, and what did you learn from the experience?**

   Things to Consider: What obstacle in your life could showcase qualities like resilience, determination, and humility? This essay should reflect your response, outlook, and demeanor when presented with one of life's challenges, rather than a detailed account of the challenge itself. That is, how do you deal with hardship?

3. **Reflect on a time when you questioned or challenged a belief or an idea. What prompted your thinking? What**

was the outcome?

Things to Consider: When has your opinion been unpopular? What makes you the kind of person who is willing to stand up for what you believe in? What is important to you on a fundamental level of morals and values? How passionate are you about the things you believe in?

4. **Describe a problem you've solved or a problem you'd like to solve. It can be an intellectual challenge, a research query, an ethical dilemma—anything that is of personal importance, no matter the scale. Explain its significance to you and what steps you took or could be taken to identify a solution.**

Things to Consider: Think about an issue or a problem that matters to you. When have you been proactive in attempting to effect change? What inspires you to take action? What kind of mark would you like to leave on the world? What problems does the future hold for you personally or globally? How might you be part of meaningful progress and problem-solving moving forward?

5. **Discuss an accomplishment, event, or realization that sparked a period of personal growth and a new understanding of yourself or others.**

Things to Consider: Think about the moments of your life that fundamentally changed you as a person. It could be a formal event or an accomplishment or perhaps a less formal event, such as meeting a special person or going on a hike or a trip to somewhere new. How did you change as a result? How do you react to periods of transition? What ideas, experiences, people inspire you to change your perspective?

6. **Describe a topic, idea, or concept you find so engaging that it makes you lose all track of time. Why does it captivate you? What or who do you turn to when you want to learn more?**

Things to Consider: Think about a class or an academic club or a summer program you've been involved in. Was there an assignment or project that really fascinated you? Think about a subject area you have explored on your own. How did you go about educating yourself without the guidance of a formal class? What lengths have you gone to in order to acquire knowledge?

7. **Share an essay on any topic of your choice. It can be one you've already written, one that responds to a different prompt, or one of your own design.**

Things to Consider: What would you want an admissions officer to know about you that they wouldn't be able to glean from your transcript, test scores, or teacher recommendations? What are the stories you continually tell your friends and family that give insight into who you are and what is important to you? What would you bring to a college campus that no one else would or could?

Sample Common App personal essay

4. *Describe a problem you've solved or a problem you'd like to solve. It can be an intellectual challenge, a research query, an ethical dilemma—anything that is of personal importance, no matter the scale. Explain its significance to you and what steps you took or could be taken to identify a solution.*

Nudging my way through the crowded campus quad at the end of January of sophomore year, I watched other students pore over my scandal-filled article. They were shocked by what they learned, and I was surprised as well, though perhaps not all for the same reasons.

Over the months leading up to the distribution of that newspaper, I investigated a story about the administration's cover-up of a wrestling coach's relationship with a student. Each new piece of information unearthed through phone calls to the city police and emails to the school administration drew me deeper into this puzzle in search of truth. Yet, after my hard work had been published, something wasn't sitting right with me. I found students catapulting vulgar comments of disgust and hatred towards the school administration, campus, and system—comments that strayed from the contents of my article. Shocked and disheartened, I realized that a project I had passionately embarked upon solely to share the truth had become a venomous wedge that drove itself deeply between the student body and our school.

It hurt that this was precisely the type of story that generated readership; the public and the newspaper had both come to prioritize criticism over connection, and controversy over community. In the following months, I continued to write for the newspaper but deliberately pursued a different mindset and focus. I documented cultural fairs, interviewed retiring teachers, chronicled park cleanups, and approached strangers to start conversations. I wanted to capture the beauty of these genuine, personal stories for other people— the kind of stories that bring out the silver lining of our community.

The following summer, as I reflected upon my school year, I was plagued by a question: *What are you bothered by and what have you done to change it?* I knew with certainty what had been gnawing at my heart, but I was also confronted with a realization—I wasn't doing enough to make the tangible impact I wanted to see. Beyond simply sharing stories, I wanted to facilitate healthy conversations about the world we live in. Inspired to take action, I called up a few international friends I had met at a business program earlier that summer and eagerly shared my ideas. From there, our journey with Quark Magazine began.

As a founding team from Canada and both US coasts, we sought via numerous animated Skype discussions and debates to ambitiously piece together a narrative that could share our passions across STEM, English, and our communities with others on a global scale. As I now edit the fascinating articles submitted by our Quark writers, I know we are creating a medium that does more than just thrive off of controversy. By addressing topics that range anywhere from the repercussions of Adderall drug abuse amongst high school students, to the translation of the physics research behind the 2017 Nobel Prize into layman's terms, we are encouraging healthy dialogues about both the ugly and beautiful facets of our world.

When I first started Quark Magazine, I never intentionally designed it as a political statement against the toxic polarization of ideas that currently permeates our country. Yet, our arrival on the journalism scene could not have been more timely: now more than ever, we must consciously promote discussions that celebrate our similarities instead of those that widen our differences. Having been a writer invested in a story of scandal, I understand the importance of exposing truths to the public. But I also believe that I can use my words, passions, and actions to turn the conversation into one not about "us versus them," but simply about "us," thus promoting more constructive responses even to cases of controversy. In the future, there will always be more scandals to be uncovered, more issues to be wrestled with, and more dialogues to be sparked. I know that I can make a difference in that plot, one story at a time.

What makes this essay good?

What makes this essay compelling isn't so much about the author's accomplishments. Notice that the essay is not just a description of the events. In fact, the essay does not go into that specific of details about what actually happened. Instead, the author decides to focus on how she feels and thinks about her accomplishments, what she hoped to achieve by starting Quark Magazine, and what she hopes to continue to achieve in her academic career. Rather than go into the details about the article she wrote or the technicalities of starting a magazine, she goes into how she reacted to the response her article elicited from the community and the goals she aspired to afterwards. In effect, it is a story about what she values as a writer, a journalist, and a human.

Bringing it all together

The college application process can be rigorous and time consuming and, yes, overwhelming. The best way to ease the pain is by getting and staying organized and, most importantly, starting early. While the Common App will help keep you organized, the onus is on you to make sure you're satisfying all the requirements. I have had some students in the past realize at the last minute they forgot to do a section of the application or not realize there was another essay requirement. Don't let this be you. The best applications tend to come from students who start early (that is, in summer) and draft their essays multiple times. This should not come as a huge surprise. I do, however, understand that a majority of high school students are excellent procrastinators, which is why I recommend to all my students these four basic steps.

- *Start small* - Start by creating a Common App account and adding all your colleges to the dashboard.

- *Get sorted* - Go through all of the supplemental requirements for each college, along with the Common App application requirements.

- *Keep organized* - Create a folder in your Google Drive to keep all your college application materials. Create sub-folders for each college you are applying to. Store your college essay requirements here.

- *Start writing* - If you feel the Common App Personal Essay is too daunting a task, start with some essays that you think would be easy or more fun or more light-hearted to write. Build your confidence.

Once you've knocked out the easy tasks, you will start building momentum. Don't let that momentum go to waste. If you get burnt out on writing essays, do some busy work. Fill out the personal information, input your grades, research some of your colleges. Keep working.

The main takeaways

- DO start early in the college application process and take your time to go over all the details.
- DO research the schools you want to apply to so you can write a good supplement.
- DO write an essay that is as representative of you as possible but also distinctive.
- DO elaborate on your thoughts, feelings, and reflections in your essays.
- DON'T assume that the Common Application will provide all the necessary or even correct information about a college's requirements.
- DON'T recycle essays without first re-tailoring them for their new prompts.
- DON'T procrastinate.

The Coalition for Access, Affordability, and Success (CAAS): What Is It, and Should I Use It?

by Ren-Horng "The Hollywood Writer"

In 2016, a new college application platform CAAS (or Coalition) debuted to give students and colleges more options in how students are admitted. This chapter will cover reasons why the Coalition came into being, its features, how it differs from the Common Application, and its essay prompts to help students decide which platform to use when applying to colleges.

Wait, there's another application platform? Why?

In the early 2000s, when colleges were switching from paper to electronic applications and looking for ways to increase their applicant pool and selectivity, many schools joined the Common Application. For a long time now, the Common Application has been the biggest game in town, and even schools that had held out against the Common Application (such as the University of Chicago and it's "Uncommon Application") folded their cards and stopped resisting.

As applying to college became standardized, a sizeable number of colleges have become increasingly unhappy with the process. Colleges have tried to break the monopoly through attempts such as the Universal Application (which had 77 members in 2010 but only 23 in 2017), and schools such as MIT, UIUC, and Virginia

Tech have been sticking to their own applications. The overall trend of the college application process, however, has been that the Common Application has crowded out every other option on the college application market.

With this in mind, in 2015, a group of leading colleges and universities came together to form the Coalition for Access, Affordability, and Success (CAAS, also "the Coalition" or "MyCoalition") as an alternative. One of CAAS's founding institutions, Harvard, also released a report in early 2016 titled "Turning the Tide: Inspiring Concern for Others and the Common Good through College Admissions", which outlines its reasons for why a new platform was necessary.

Primarily, the top colleges in the U.S. were becoming concerned that the criteria being used to admit students had become too focused on individual achievement and not enough on the quality of the character of the applicant. Additionally, the Coalition's founding members wanted to make applying to college more affordable and accessible for lower-income students.

Of course, grades, test scores, and individual achievements are still important, but with CAAS, schools are hoping to use a more holistic assessment of applicants by giving students the opportunity to provide supplemental materials and start planning for college as early as 9th grade.

Does that mean that colleges will prefer the Coalition Application?

Not necessarily. While colleges may appreciate that you are "in the know" on the latest trends in the college application process, these schools are also aware that not everyone will have equal access to information, and school counselors in different places might be slow to get the word on these changes. Furthermore, if colleges wanted their students to use the Coalition application only, then they wouldn't give students the option of either the Common App or Coalition in the first place.

That being said, as Coalition is a new platform, some kinks and bugs in the system are still being worked out. As such, some Coalition members such as UIUC and Penn State give students the option of using their own applications instead of the Coalition application. Many schools are on both the Common Application and Coalition, and schools that are members of both are likely to stay members of both for the foreseeable future.

Facts about the Coalition for Access, Affordability, and Success

As of April 2018, CAAS had 140+ member schools. Its membership criteria are as follows:

- Affordable tuition
- Provide need-based aid
- Have a six-year graduation rate of 70% or higher
- 1 Essay approx. 450-550 words

The Coalition website itself recommends 500-550 words for its essay, which is the official "soft" limit, but schools like the University of Washington may cap the essay with a hard limit of 500 words. Other schools like the University of Illinois Urbana-Champaign may not even ask for the general Coalition essay and only require students answer the school-specific questions. The Coalition provides greater flexibility for the college in determining what goes into their application, but this might lead to some confusion with prospective students.

CAAS features

The Locker

The Locker is a space that allows students to build a portfolio of their best essays, paintings, and other projects throughout high school. This space is private to the student unless the student wishes to share certain files with a counselor, collaborator, or college admissions officer. Unless the student chooses to share a file, s/he does not need to worry that a college will see anything that is not yet ready or not of top quality.

This space becomes available to students as early as 9th grade and can be used without applying to college that year. Having a log of achievements online will come in handy when trying to craft a resume or list of accomplishments to apply to college, particularly for students who may have trouble remembering what they did last week.

The Coalition touts that the Locker has an individual file size limit of 50 MB, but storage is unlimited. However, none of my students have yet pushed this feature to its limit!

Collaboration Space

The Collaboration Space allows students to connect digitally with mentors of their choice (for example, teachers, counselors, coaches, parents, or family friends) and ask for advice, recommendations, and feedback on the college application process. This space is meant to encourage students to have meaningful conversations with trusted adults to help guide them to college success.

This component is integrated with the student's Locker, allowing the student to share items from his or her Locker, such as a college list, an essay, or piece of artwork with mentors and seek their opinion. Mentors can only see and comment on items that students have invited them to view. Mentors cannot make changes to items in a student's Locker.

In the secure Collaboration Space, students are encouraged to seek feedback and advice from mentors that can have a direct impact on their success in the college admissions process.

MyCoalition Counselor

Just by signing up for CAAS, students have access to free resources on choosing colleges, financial aid, and tips written by college admissions counselors themselves. These resources are articles, so unfortunately, students do not have direct access to admissions counselors for advice outside of students emailing individual college's admissions offices. Of course, the college admissions counselors who have contributed articles to this section of CAAS may provide information that's more helpful to the specific college that they work for, which may or may not be your dream school, so your mileage with their advice may vary.

This portion is hidden under "Help" in the upper right-hand corner of the Coalition page once you log in, so this resource might not be readily apparent for most students when logging in.

Application Portal

The Coalition's application is designed to minimize stress, confusion, and intimidation. In theory, it encourages universities to ask questions that will reveal students with the greatest fit for their campuses. In practice, however, for the past few years, the individual school questions for colleges that are on both the Coalition and Common Application have been the same. This mirroring of individual school questions on both platforms is likely to continue for the foreseeable future, with the main difference being the two platforms' different prompts and lengths for the main, shared essay.

CAAS vs. Common App

CAAS	Common App
• Goal is to increase applicant diversity	• Accepted by more universities
• Students can get feedback about their application from mentors via the Locker	• Mostly for Senior year applicants, although students can set up account junior year
• Students start planning for college early (9th grade)	• Less likely to have glitches
• 1 essay 450-550 words	• 1 essay 650 words max

The Coalition essay prompts

1. Tell a story from your life, describing an experience that either demonstrates your character or helped to shape it.

This prompt is very broad, so consider the following:

- Choose a story that demonstrates *character.*

- How do you see yourself? Are you resilient? Outgoing? Courageous?
- What are the characteristics that form the foundation to your personality?
- Describe a specific experience that demonstrates the character you want admissions to know.
- This prompt is similar to the Common App prompt #1.

2. Describe a time when you made a meaningful contribution to others in which the greater good was your focus. Discuss the challenges and rewards of making your contribution.

This prompt provides the opportunity to write about any volunteering activities you have participated in; however, keep the following in mind:

- It's best to write about an experience you followed up on.
- Choose a small moment within a larger experience.
- Include highly personalized details of how you made an impact and how the experience helped shape you.
- Make sure the impact you made is meaningful.
- This prompt can be tied to an experience/problem you chose for the Common App prompt #4.

3. Has there been a time when you've had a long-cherished or accepted belief challenged? How did you respond? How did the challenge affect your beliefs?

This prompt requires a great deal of introspection and provides an opportunity to show growth and development. Consider the following:

- The belief chosen can be something acquired from parents or something absorbed from your daily life.
- In general, avoid controversial subjects such as politics.
- Illustrate the effect the experience had on you and how this has contributed to who you are *today.*

- This prompt is the *opposite* of Common App #3.

4. What is the hardest part of being a teenager now? What's the best part? What advice would you give a younger sibling or friend (assuming they would listen to you)?

This prompt provides an opportunity to be a bit more light-hearted and fun compared to the others. Consider the following:

- Make sure your essay is unique and highly personal, especially if you choose a common problem facing teens (i.e. bullying, peer pressure).
- Be specific in the advice you choose to offer.
- Remember that the essay is about *you* and not teenage life in general.
- This prompt could be tied in to Common App prompts #1 and #5.

5. Submit an essay on a topic of your choice.

This prompt provides an opportunity to be creative. You literally can choose/create any prompt you want. Consider the following:

- Choose a prompt that illustrates something about *you* that admissions won't see any place else in your application.
- Remember, the story you tell is what is important, not the prompt.
- Any of the Common App prompts can be used here, as long as they are within the word limit.

Sample essay

Although E. was born in America, she was raised in China up until it was time for her to attend school. Throughout her childhood, she was very shy and often felt like she did not fit in. To make matters more difficult for E., she lost a very close family member at a young age. Determined to help others, throughout high school, she volunteered for numerous organizations and events. She enlisted in competitions ranging from violin to the Intel International Science and Engineering Fair. Working toward her dream to find a cure for cancer, she got involved with research via an internship at Boston University. E.'s immediate goals are to obtain a B.S. in chemistry and ultimately, to pursue a career in pharmacology, specializing in oncology.

1. Tell a story from your life, describing an experience that either demonstrates your character or helped to shape it.

Prowling down the halls, dressed all in black with wooden sword in hand, I was the perfect ninja chasing after a thief. Knowing my Barbies were in the hands of my troublemaking sister, I rushed to rescue them from harm. We wrestled back and forth, ending with the Barbies cradled in my arms. Yet, this isn't the first time I put on my ninja gear to save those in need. From the moment I laid eyes on those stealthy warriors fighting evil and saving lives, I was convinced being a ninja was my life's calling. However, troubles kept standing in my way.

"Ninjas are known for being highly intelligent, honey"- Mom

My first challenge was my label of "English Learner." As a child growing up in a Chinese household, with both parents speaking Chinese to me, kindergarten was the first time I was exposed to English. Throughout the years, I heard hushed whispers now and then, voicing their disbelief in my academic career and my ninja dreams. But I refused to give up. I'd dive into books, sounding out unknown words and learning idioms. I'd scour dictionaries, trying to perfectly translate that Chinese word. I'd buy workbooks, completing problem after problem until my hands cramped and eyes drooped. Rather than giving up or feeling discouraged, I used my difficulties as motivation, not allowing my circumstances to define me. Even if I had to work twice as hard as others to achieve the same results, I was willing to put in the extra work. Through perseverance and determination, I changed from the girl who couldn't write her name without squinting at her nametag to the girl who could win debates with eloquently articulated arguments. I have developed into a person who will continually attempt to achieve the "impossible," no matter the challenges and difficulties that stand in my way.

"You still can't be a ninja. It's not legal," my mom sighed after I ordered a samurai sword off the internet and started swinging it around.

As I grew older, I started to see the multitude of obstacles preventing me from becoming one of those brave warriors; mainly, the legality of walking in the streets with sword in the air, even if it was for saving lives. So, I put my ninja future on hold, but I never lost hope because of the determination and tenacity learned from childhood.

Whether it was auditioning for the Morning Glow Gu Zheng Ensemble or coaxing an autistic girl out of her shell, I continued to apply the same mentality and energy I applied to learning English. I entered History Bowl Competitions and published science articles, never forgetting my childhood dream. However, I found myself gravitating towards science and diseases. As I matured, I realized more ways to save lives exist. I don't need to fight with a sword to make a difference— research and science can too.

Even if I can't be a sword swinging ninja, I'm still a true ninja at heart because I embody the qualities and values that ninjas represent. Along my journey to become one, I learned hard work and determination. I learned to fight challenges with perseverance and confidence. I learned hope. I know with these attributes, I can accomplish anything I desire—my dream of helping others.

As you can see, the structure of a Coalition essay isn't that different from a Common App essay. In fact, her Common App essay told the same story. Therefore, find a story to tell isn't the challenging part; rather, the biggest challenge for most students is often trying to shave a story down to 550 (or even 500!) words.

Is the Coalition right for me?

You will also find that some popular schools that are on the Common Application have decided NOT to join the Coalition as of 2018, including but not limited to:

- Barnard College
- Boston College
- Carnegie Mellon University
- New York University
- Tulane University
- University of Southern California

If you plan to apply to these schools, you will still need to apply through the Common Application. Conversely, some popular schools that have never been on the Common Application have joined the Coalition and will now allow you to apply to many of them with one application. These schools include but are not limited to:

- Penn State
- University of Illinois at Urbana Champaign
- University of Texas at Austin
- University of Washington - Seattle
- Virginia Tech

And then there's some colleges that aren't on either and have decided to stick with their own applications:

- Massachusetts Institute of Technology
- Georgetown University

Faced with these choices, your decision should then be based on what is the most time efficient for you. If you have more schools that are Common Application only, then use the Common

Application. If you have more schools that are Coalition only, then use the Coalition. Of course, if your list has a mix of schools that are only on Common App and Coalition, then you'll still have to use both.

However, if all of your schools give you the option of either, then consider: What features of which application platforms do you like? Are their quirks of certain platforms that you don't like? From there, picking your application platform is a matter of personal fit.

Bringing it all together

The Coalition for Access, Affordability, and Success (CAAS or the Coalition) provides students and colleges an alternative to the Common Application. Familiarizing yourself with the features of CAAS, its requirements, and which schools are members can help you decide which platform to use when you apply to college. Individual schools may have different requirements, but the long essay will be similar in structure and purpose to the Common App essay but shorter.

The main takeaways

- DO research which schools are on CAAS and/or Common App.
- DO familiarize yourself with the features of CAAS and take advantage of them.
- DO pay attention to specific school requirements and deadlines.
- DO make a school list to decide which application platform is most time efficient for you.
- DON'T assume all member schools have the same requirements.
- DON'T ignore requirements specific to particular member schools.

Appendix: Sample Essays

Harvard Common App Essay

With gloves on and shovels in our hands, cracked, dry earth underneath and blazing sun above, we pair up to dig the foundation holes to erect greenhouses. I begin thrusting my shovel to break up the hard and dry soil. At times, I also have to kneel onto the ground to remove the caving dirt with my hands.

When I originally signed up to volunteer on this Environmental Policy project in a remote village in China for this summer, I did not have a clearly identified problem or issue, let alone any concrete solutions to the challenges we face today. Yet as I researched more about the remote village in Ningxia, I began to see real-world examples of the concepts of artificial scarcity and rational ignorance in my economics studies.

With minutes turning into hours, my aching arms and knees finally get to rest when some village children call us for a lunch break at their homes. We go directly back to our hostess, Wang Lanlan's house. My curiosity takes me into her kitchen, where Lanlan is pressing handmade noodles in a murky tub of water. My inquiry about the water only receives a terse replay from Lanlan: "Water is very precious."

Several days later, a light rain comes down around lunchtime; Lanlan's three kids immediately run out to set buckets and pans to collect the rain drops. She smiles, first time her face lighting up truly since we came to the village. In this part of the world, rainfall is so scarce that any water has become such a precious commodity. Villagers like the Wang's no longer have enough water to even satisfy their basic daily needs; rather, water is a political chip for government officials to haggle about and trade with for each other's favors. What a raw demonstration of the economic principles of rational ignorance and the incentives that drive the Ningxia government agencies to shortchange their own, poor villagers!

Many of society's great challenges today point to complex causes and even more complicated solutions, if there were any at all. But that doesn't mean I give up trying. Appreciating first hand these farmers' struggles of living their lives with limited and, in most cases and on most days, dirty and unfiltered water, I take my participation in the greenhouse construction project even more seriously. Every one of the eighty-two holes required for building each of the 8-by-40-meter greenhouses that I dug, along with every 8-by-3-meter tall steel-frame I helped erect, represent part of a small but concrete step towards crafting a sustainable, pragmatic solution to improve the villagers' lives.

In the evenings when we reflect about our undertakings in the village, I am appalled to realize more examples from my economics textbooks. The Ningxia farmers enjoy cheap and plentiful electricity at home; however, the local governments restrict any rerouting of grid power to agricultural applications. This practice has resulted in the Yellow-River-sourced irrigation only going to state-owned plantations. The resulting, artificial scarcity of both agricultural electricity and water has forced some villagers to abandon farming altogether. Some years they do not even have enough drinking water!

Hence, we do not just stop at building greenhouses. Some of my group is more engineering inclined students are developing a wind-and-solar powered control system to efficiently irrigate the greenhouse fields. When one of the hot-spot devices for remotely monitoring the power systems burned out, I even join the debugging effort by adding my expertise about the Internet-cloud-based Power

Logger. In the end, the team circumvented the unfair government regulations on electricity.

My Ningxia experience has certainly shown me that any economic and technological solutions to address society's issues remain challenging and complex. It has also inspired me to further pursue the studies of political economics and public policies and, ultimately, to reform public policy at its economic core—saying goodbyes to both artificial scarcity and rational ignorance.

Commentary

Many high school students seem to think that writing about a volunteering trip alone will grant them admission to their dream school, but what's far more important than bragging about having gone on such a trip is the meaning the student gains from the experience. In writing an essay that is more than the mere appreciation for the comforts of home in an impoverished country, M. shows his understanding that many issues cannot be solved just through simple charity; rather, problems with complex causes may also need equally complex solutions. M. is also able to elegantly tie together the course material he is learning in school with the activities of the trip and his future ambitions. This ability to apply academic knowledge and synthesize concepts shows a high level of thinking top colleges appreciate, as they want students who will be able to piece together different fields of knowledge to devise new solutions to age-old problems. M.'s chronicle of his experience and ability to connect concepts show great promise in his future goals to pursue political economics and public policy, making him a desirable candidate for admission.

Princeton Supplemental Essay

Using the statement below as a starting point, tell us about an event or experience that helped you define one of your values or changed how you approach the world. "Princeton in the Nation's Service" was the title of a speech given by Woodrow Wilson on the 150th anniversary of the University. It became the unofficial Princeton motto and was expanded for the University's 250th anniversary to "Princeton in the nation's service and in the service of all nations." - Woodrow Wilson, Princeton Class of 1879, served on the faculty and was Princeton's president from 1902–1910.

For a moment, I feel as though I am a part of the community. As I paint Jupiter, smudging brown against hues of yellow and orange, a girl my age, Tierra, tells me about her tabby cat.

However, when she finishes and asks, "*Why* exactly are you here?" I am out of the community again.

Before I can answer, a boy passing us says, "She's in the service group."

And with that, Tierra grows more reserved and I am just part of the one-week service group that volunteers at the after school youth center. In a few weeks, Tierra may only remember me as the "artistically-challenged girl from California who led art activities." To some, I'll become another "one-week girl."

For a week at the Whiteriver Apache Reservation in Arizona, I cultivated my inner artist and coordinated activities. Under the shade of a tree buzzing with cicadas, I sat alone at the crafts table with nail polish, bracelets, and bags. "Do you want to do crafts?" I'd call out to every passerby. "Not really my thing," some responded. But most did not notice or ignored my calls. Swatting flies away from my face in the stagnant summer, I felt foreign.

Service has always been my way of connecting with the community, whether at school, home, or the places I've visited. When I volunteered in these communities, there was always the perfect combination of being welcomed, connecting with people, and seeing the impact I had made. I wasn't out to change the world, but I needed to know I was doing something.

My trip to Arizona, however, showed me that service is not always the feel-good experience I had always believed in. Instead, I was met with distant glances and hushed whispers. I had expected to implement change in the community, but I was disappointed. By the end of the week, not only had I not done anything, but also I felt uncomfortable whenever someone mentioned my name with service. I wanted to connect with people, not simply be known as a "one-week girl."

The label "service" limited the depth of my connections with them. When people sat at the crafts table, they usually asked, "When are you leaving?" I answered quietly, not wanting to be defined by how long I stayed. While I sat alone at the crafts table, I realized that service is much more than just spending a week, or two, or even months, in a place. I wanted to reach beyond that barrier and connect with them. Part of service is doing the act, but for me, the more important component is bonding with people across different cultures and communities. In wanting to build those connections, I will inevitably continue to face service's complexities and the different ways that it is perceived. Service is multifaceted, more than just an activity in a foreign place or an extension of what I do. I want service to be such a fundamental part of who I am that I feel so immersed in it, *I* forget that it is service. I want everyone, including myself, to believe I am more than just another "one-week girl."

Commentary

What makes F.'s piece a winning essay is not just that she has done many service activities, which are impressive in their own right, but that she also demonstrates complex thought and maturity by acknowledging that "doing good" is not all she can contribute. F. shows her understanding that connecting with the people she serves provides greater meaning not just for herself but also appreciation from the people she interacts with. She recognizes that the people she helps have their own needs and wants and are not just objects for others to help, thus making the effort to interact with them as equals. She also acknowledges that input from locals is required to solve problems with complex roots instead of being an outsider who claims to know better than the locals. This kind of deep thinking and reflection for further future problem solving, instead of a self-congratulatory pat on the back for doing a good deed, shows her potential to be a thoughtful and empathetic leader, the kind of person that a top school wants as a student.

Made in the USA
Las Vegas, NV
05 July 2021

25971674R00115